T0041712

SOCIALISM 101

FROM **THE BOLSHEVIKS** AND **KARL MARX** TO **UNIVERSAL HEALTHCARE AND THE DEMOCRATIC SOCIALISTS, EVERYTHING YOU NEED TO KNOW ABOUT SOCIALISM**

KATHLEEN SEARS

Adams Media

New York London Toronto Sydney New Delhi

Adams Media
An Imprint of Simon & Schuster, Inc.
100 Technology Center Drive
Stoughton, MA 02072

First Adams Media hardcover edition September 2019

ADAMS MEDIA and colophon are trademarks of Simon & Schuster.

For information about special discounts for bulk purchases, please contact Simon &
Schuster Special Sales at 1-866-506-1949 or business@simonandschuster.com.

The Simon & Schuster Speakers Bureau can bring authors to your live event. For more
information or to book an event contact the Simon & Schuster Speakers Bureau at
1-866-248-3049 or visit our website at www.simonspeakers.com.

Manufactured in the United States of America

2 2022

Library of Congress Cataloging-in-Publication Data has been applied for.

ISBN 978-1-5072-1136-6
ISBN 978-1-5072-1137-3 (ebook)

Contains material adapted from the following title published by Adams Media, an
Imprint of Simon & Schuster, Inc.: *The Everything® Guide to Understanding Socialism*
by Pamela D. Toler, PhD, copyright © 2011, ISBN 978-1-4405-1277-3.

CONTENTS

INTRODUCTION

Have you ever wondered just what people mean when they use the word *socialism*? Are you curious about the different kinds of socialism—from Marxism to democratic socialism to the British welfare state? Do you want to know the long tradition of socialist thought, in both Europe and America?

If so, *Socialism 101* is for you. Here you'll learn, in clear, simple language, where socialism started, how it's changed over the years, and what it means today. You'll find entries that cover such topics as:

- Who were Karl Marx and Friedrich Engels, founders of "scientific socialism"?
- How did socialists, led by Vladimir Lenin, take power in Russia in 1917?
- What does "democratic socialism" mean, and how is it different from Marxist socialism?
- What do today's socialist politicians want?

Socialism has entered the political dialogue today, and it's important to know more about it. Like many political terms, it's heavily charged and often misunderstood. But increasingly voters are being given choices of electing socialist, or socialist-leaning, candidates. More and more people are open to socialism and want to understand it. Part of the problem is that a lot of people aren't sure where to start. As with many things, it's a good idea to begin by learning where socialism came from and what its creators were trying to say.

Some people think socialism is a recent creation. In fact, socialist ideas have been around for hundreds of years. Their roots lie back in the eighteenth century, when people first began to dispute the notion that kings had a right to rule them. Socialist thinking underwent a long evolution, stimulated by historic events, such as the European revolutions of 1848. These revolutions spurred two young men, Karl Marx and Friedrich Engels, to write a document titled *The Communist Manifesto*. Today the world is still feeling the effects of that little pamphlet.

All of this may sound a bit complicated, but this book will help you make sense of it. It gives you the historical background of where socialist ideas came from as well as clear, straightforward explanations of what the different types of socialists stood and stand for.

Socialism has had an impact on tens of millions of people over the years. Today it's seeing a resurgence. So whether you're coming to this political and economic theory for the first time or you want to brush up on your existing knowledge, in these pages you'll find helpful information to put socialism in its historical and political context. Now let's get started.

WHAT IS SOCIALISM?

Beginning with the Basics

It seems as if every day someone is denouncing (or sometimes complimenting) someone else with the label of *socialist*. Yet these people often believe completely different things. Surely they can't *all* be socialists, can they?

Clearly, the word *socialism* means different things to different people. The definition of socialism has been stretched very far, but it usually includes a few core beliefs.

CAPITALISM VERSUS SOCIALISM

Socialism is an economic and political system that's usually put forward as an alternative to or modification of capitalism, the system under which a majority of the world's countries live. This is one reason that a lot of socialist writing deals with capitalism at least as much as socialism. Karl Marx (1818–1883), the most important theoretician of socialist ideology, wrote a three-volume book called *Capital*, devoted to explaining exactly how capitalism works.

Under capitalism, goods and services are produced socially, but they and the wealth they generate are owned privately. For example, if you were to visit a car factory, you wouldn't see each worker constructing only one car, building it from scratch, from engine to lug nuts. Rather, you'd see the workers laboring together, each one performing a different task, or series of tasks, to help create the final product: a car.

But when the car makes its way to a dealership and is sold, the profit realized isn't sent back to the factory to be divided among the workers. It goes to whoever owns the factory—in this case, the shareholders, people who bought stock in the company. The largest shareholders realize the greatest amount of profit.

Many Different Capitalisms

Just as there are different varieties of socialism, so are there many types of capitalism. In mid-nineteenth-century Britain (the place Karl Marx wrote about in *Capital*) capitalism was largely unregulated. Workers, including young children, worked long hours in highly unsafe conditions and often died in industrial accidents or of diseases brought on by foul working conditions and poor nutrition. Gradually, as you'll see in the following pages, workers were able to change many of these conditions and fight for shorter hours and better pay. But the more regulated capitalism seen during the twentieth and twenty-first centuries is still capitalism.

Socialists—and we'll see that the currents of thought that eventually coalesced into socialist ideas go back many centuries—believe that goods and services that are produced socially should be *owned* socially. Such goods and services should not be created for private profit but for public good, administered through the state. In this way, the state becomes a means of social equality and justice.

This isn't to say that socialists believe you shouldn't be able to own your own toothbrush or live in your own house (although there have been some extreme societies, such as Pol Pot's Cambodia in the 1970s, that tried to enforce such rigid regulations). For socialists it's the larger goods and services that should be owned and administered in common.

SOME EXAMPLES OF
SOCIALIZED PROPERTY

Examples of property administered by the state in the interests of the entire population are easy to find. In many countries, including the United States, rail services such as Amtrak are public corporations (there are also private rail companies, such as Union Pacific Railroad and Norfolk Southern Railway). Amtrak has often suffered from issues with funding, since its funds come from the government. But it's essentially a national rail system for the United States.

Healthcare is another example. Medicare and Medicaid in the US are socialized healthcare, in which the government pays the majority of health expenses for older and indigent patients. The National Health Service in the UK goes even further, paying the overwhelming majority of healthcare expenses for British citizens. While the program does suffer from problems, it's an example of how a socialized system can work. In fact, a majority of first-world countries have some form of socialized healthcare.

Healthcare Around the World

The UK isn't the only place where you'll find socialized healthcare. Countries with some form of national healthcare include Mexico, Cuba, Canada, Egypt, Morocco, South Africa, Israel, Japan, China, Australia, New Zealand, and almost all of the countries in Europe.

Socialism also often implies a political approach to social change. Some socialists believe in gradual reforms and legislation to implement aspects of socialism. Others argue that capitalists will never give up their power willingly and therefore a revolution is necessary. Both approaches have been tried, with varying results.

SOCIALISM'S FAILURES

Opponents of socialism point to its failures:

- In the former Soviet Union an overly planned economy resulted in inefficiencies, lack of consumer goods, and agricultural disasters that led to famines that killed millions. An oppressive government imprisoned or killed many of its citizens until the state collapsed abruptly in 1991.
- China's revolution of 1949 brought to power a ruling elite that nationalized property and collectivized agriculture. But as in the USSR mistakes and miscalculations resulted in disasters such as the Great Leap Forward, in which millions perished. Today some socialist property forms exist alongside limited capitalist investment.
- Cuba's 1959 revolution resulted in better healthcare for the population and a literacy rate higher than any in the Caribbean or Central America. But the state has been largely oppressive, leading hundreds of thousands to flee their homeland.

Whether these failures expose some fundamental flaw of socialist theory or they mark the outcome of particular circumstances and historical conditions is widely debated. Some people argue that even the Soviet Union was not truly socialist but rather a form of state-run capitalism. They conclude that a true socialist society has yet to be implemented. Others heatedly dispute this conclusion.

This book doesn't aim to convince you of one position or the other. Instead, we want to help you understand what socialist ideas are and what they imply for the future. To grasp the full meaning of socialism, we must look at its beginnings, which are deeply rooted in the past.

THE BEGINNINGS OF SOCIALIST THOUGHT

The Forerunners

In the sixteenth century the economics of Europe began to change. The complicated structure of rights and duties that made up the feudal system was slowly being replaced by a market economy organized on the basis of personal gain. New freedoms were accompanied by new hardships—and new social disorder. Concerned with the contrast between what was and what ought to be, political philosophers, beginning with Sir Thomas More, struggled to understand the nature of a just, stable, and efficient society. In the process they laid the foundations for later socialist thought.

SIR THOMAS MORE INVENTS UTOPIA

Sir Thomas More (1478–1535) wrote during a time when England was in political, cultural, and intellectual turmoil. Tudor England was an age of flourishing Renaissance culture and the transformative effect of the Reformation. It was also a period of political conflict and plunder. During his reign King Henry VIII seized land from Catholic monasteries and distributed it to his supporters. Others competed for patronage from the Crown in the form of jobs, lands, pensions, and annuities.

The son of a prominent lawyer and judge, More studied at Oxford for two years until 1494, when his father called him back to London to study common law. By 1515, when he began to write his most famous work, *Utopia*, he was a successful lawyer and held a seat in

Parliament. He devoted his leisure time to scholarship, becoming part of the international fraternity of northern humanists led by the radical Catholic theologian Desiderius Erasmus.

Humanists and the Renaissance

Humanist philosophers of the fifteenth and sixteenth centuries turned to the classical texts of Greece and Rome as a way of understanding man's life on earth. Northern humanists also used their Greek to study the New Testament and the works of leading saints of the church as part of a campaign to reform the Catholic Church from within.

In 1515 More traveled to Bruges, the capital of West Flanders in Belgium, as part of a trade delegation. His discussions with Erasmus and other humanist scholars while in Flanders inspired him to write the political tract that earned him a permanent place in the history of thought: *A Pamphlet truly Golden no less beneficial than enjoyable concerning the republic's best state and concerning the new Island Utopia*, better known simply as *Utopia*.

More and King Henry VIII

More's other claim to fame was his refusal to support Henry VIII's divorce from Catherine of Aragon and subsequent marriage to Anne Boleyn. More saw both acts as an assault on the church; the king saw More's refusal as treason. More was tried and executed on July 6, 1535. He was canonized by Pope Pius XI 400 years later.

Published in the city of Leuven in 1516, the book was an immediate success with its intended audience: More's fellow humanists and the elite circle of public officials whom he soon joined. The book went quickly into several editions and was soon translated from Latin into most European languages.

The Society of Utopia

More's *Utopia* is divided into two parts. The first part is written in the form of a dialogue between More and an imaginary traveler who has recently returned from newly discovered lands, including the island nation of Utopia. In comparing the traveler's accounts of the imaginary countries he visited with the actual countries of sixteenth-century Europe, More criticizes the social conditions of his day, particularly what he describes as "acquisitiveness" and "retaining" on the part of the wealthy and the "terrible necessity of hunger" that drove the poor to crimes against society.

In the second half of the tract More describes in detail the social, political, economic, and religious conditions of an imaginary society on the island of Utopia.

A Place Too Good to Be True

More created a new word to describe his ideal community, combining the Greek negative *ou* with *topos* ("place") to create *utopia*, "no place"—a pun on *eu-topos*, "good place." The term *utopia* is now used to describe a place too good to be real. In 1868 John Stuart Mill created its antonym, *dystopia*, to describe a place too bad to exist.

Like later reformers who shared his concerns about the negative effects of urbanization and industrialism, More proposed a small agrarian community as the prototype for the perfect society. His goal was an egalitarian society that did away with both idleness born of wealth and excessive labor due to poverty. On the island of Utopia everyone performed useful work and everyone had time for appropriate leisure. All citizens worked on farms and in town so that all acquired skills in both agriculture and a trade. No type of work was held in higher esteem than any other, and no money was required. Each family took what they produced to one of four public markets and received what they needed in return.

There was no private property. Individual family houses were assigned every ten years by lottery. Although families were free to eat meals in their homes, most preferred to eat in the common dining halls that were shared between thirty families because eating together was more pleasant than eating alone.

The government of Utopia was a combination of republic and meritocracy, in which a select few ruled with the consent of the governed. Every citizen had a voice in government, and secret ballots were used so no man could be persecuted because of his vote. Each group of thirty families elected a magistrate (*philarch*). The magistrates chose an *archphilarch*, who in turn elected a prince. Even though all citizens had a vote, not all citizens were eligible for office. Important officials could be chosen only from a limited group, who were selected because of their superior gifts.

More's Influence on Later Thinkers

More wrote *Utopia* more than 300 years before the word *socialism* first appeared in the language of social reform. Nonetheless, early socialists found much to emulate in his writing, including:

- The abolition of private property
- The universal obligation to work

- The right to an equal share of society's wealth
- The concept of equal rights under the law
- State management and control of production

UTOPIA REVISED

James Harrington (1611–1677) was an aristocrat by birth and served as a Gentleman of the Bedchamber to King Charles I prior to and during the English Civil War. When he later wrote about the war, Harrington built his philosophical system on an examination of historical cause and effect. He came to the conclusion that the underlying cause for the Civil War, also known as the Puritan Revolution, was the uneven distribution of land ownership.

Harrington made a distinction between power and authority. Power was based on wealth, which he called the "goods of fortune," the most important of which was land. Authority was based on the "goods of the mind," namely wisdom, prudence, and courage. The best rulers combined both.

Since power was based on wealth, rather than on wisdom, property was the foundation of the state. The way property was distributed between "the one, the few, and the many" reflected the form of the government. In an absolute monarchy the balance of property was in control of one man, the king, and mercenaries maintained the rule of law.

Commonwealth of Oceana

In *Commonwealth of Oceana* (1656) Harrington proposed a social program designed to avoid the problems that led to the English Civil War. Concerned more with social order than with social justice, Harrington aimed to create a society in which "no man or men...can have the interest, or having the interest, can have the power to disturb [the commonwealth] with sedition."

Since power depends on wealth, Harrington believed that the way to ensure political stability was to prevent the concentration of property in the hands of a few families. In England the common practice of primogeniture, in which the eldest son inherits all or most of a father's property, allowed the wealthy to accumulate and transmit property, and consequently political power, from one generation to another. In *Oceana* a man's property was divided equally among his children at his death, so power remained widely distributed.

Founding Fathers Learn from Harrington

The American founding fathers studied Harrington's ideas and many of them were incorporated into the Constitution of the United States, including the bicameral Congress, the indirect election of the president, and the separation of powers.

Harrington also deterred the development of an oligarchy through a strict division of power between the legislative and executive branches of government. Power was further separated in the legislature, which was made up of two houses with distinct responsibilities. The upper chamber, called the senate after the Roman legislature, was responsible for proposing and debating policy but had no power to enact law. The lower house was responsible for voting on the policies the upper house proposed, but it was not allowed to propose or debate policy. Representatives of the upper house were drawn from a "natural aristocracy" gifted with the "goods of the mind." Representatives of the lower house were drawn from the people. Representatives of both houses were elected by indirect ballot and held their positions for fixed terms on a rotating basis. The electorate and pool from which representatives were chosen included all adult male property holders, with two exceptions.

THE NATURAL RIGHTS OF MAN

The son of an attorney who fought on the side of Parliament in the English Civil War, British philosopher John Locke (1632–1704) is often considered the first philosopher of the Enlightenment. He studied the standard classics curriculum at Oxford but was more interested in the new ideas about the nature and origin of knowledge that were developed by the natural philosophers of the sixteenth century.

In 1666 Locke found a patron: Lord Anthony Ashley Cooper, later the first Earl of Shaftesbury. Locke and Shaftesbury shared numerous political positions, including support for constitutional monarchy, the Protestant succession, civil liberties, religious tolerance, and parliamentary rule. When his patron was arrested, tried, and acquitted of treason in 1681, Locke followed him into exile in the Netherlands.

Locke wrote *Two Treatises of Government* (1689) to explain his political ideas. In the first treatise he refutes the divine right of kings. In the second Locke argues that all men are born with certain natural rights, including the right to survive and the right to have the means to survive, with the corollary obligation not to harm others. Each society creates a government to protect those rights.

Since government exists by the consent of the governed and not by the divine right of kings, citizens have the right to withdraw their consent if a government fails in its duty to protect their rights.

THE INVISIBLE HAND OF THE MARKETPLACE

One other figure should be considered important in the development of socialist thought—although oddly, he's often identified with free-market capitalism. Considered the founder of modern economics, Adam Smith (1723–1790) was an important figure in the Scottish Enlightenment. In 1776 Smith published *An Inquiry into the Nature and Causes of the Wealth of Nations*, which he intended to be the first volume of a complete theory of society. *The Wealth of Nations* was the first major work of political economy.

In this work Smith examined the market economy in detail for the first time. He overturned old ideas of wealth when he identified labor, not gold or land, as the true source of wealth. He demonstrated how the law of supply and demand regulates the prices of specific goods and examined how capital is accumulated and used. He took fascinating side excursions into the manufacture of pins, luxury goods produced under the Abbasid Caliphate (a major dynasty of the Islamic Empire), and statistics on the North Atlantic herring catch.

At its heart *The Wealth of Nations* was an attack on the dominant economic theory of the time: mercantilism. Under mercantilism, governments created elaborate systems of regulations, tariffs, and monetary controls to protect their economies. Smith proposed a free market in which the "invisible hand" of the marketplace replaces government control and brings prosperity to all, coining the word *capitalism* to distinguish it from mercantilism.

THE FOUNDATIONS OF SOCIALIST THOUGHT

The political theorists of the sixteenth and seventeenth centuries laid the foundation for later socialist thought with their enquiries into the relationship between the one, the few, and the many. Questions of equality and inequality, the distribution of wealth, the basis for authority, and the rights of man (narrowly defined) were now part of the public discourse.

THE RISE OF THE INDUSTRIAL WORKING CLASS

A Revolution from Below

Modern socialism has its roots in the mills and slums of the Industrial Revolution. The ability to make goods quickly and cheaply soared as manufacturers found more and more ways to use machines to extend the productivity of a single man. Many welcomed machines and the wealth they created as the embodiment of progress. Others were troubled by the conditions under which the new urban poor lived and worked. A few began to consider ways in which the fruits of this growth in productivity could be shared more equally.

THE EIGHTEENTH-CENTURY POPULATION EXPLOSION

After a century of virtually no population growth, the countries of Western Europe experienced dramatic population increases between 1750 and 1800. Many countries doubled in size. In some countries the growth continued through the nineteenth century. The population of Great Britain, for instance, doubled between 1750 and 1800 and then tripled between 1800 and 1900.

There were several reasons for the sudden increase. Medical advances and improved hygiene limited the devastation caused by epidemic diseases and plagues. The introduction of new food crops, most notably the potato, provided a better diet for the poor and reduced the incidence of famine. The combination of greater public order and fewer civil wars meant that life was less hazardous. The net result was a lower death rate and soaring population.

The Agricultural Revolution

The Industrial Revolution was paralleled by an agricultural revolution in Great Britain. New horse-drawn machinery, better fodder crops, extensive land drainage projects, and scientific stockbreeding increased agricultural productivity. But improved farming had a social cost. Between 1760 and 1799 large landowners fenced in between 2 and 3 million acres of common land that small farmers had previously used for grazing.

The growing population, with a rising proportion of children to raise and older people to care for, put increased pressure on every aspect of society. Many peasants were no longer able to provide land for their children, who were forced to look for other ways to make their living. Small artisans in the cities suffered similar problems, unable to provide places for their children in their own workshops. The growth in population increased the demand for both food and manufactured goods and provided an abundance of cheap labor to produce them.

WEAVING BECOMES A MODERN INDUSTRY

The Industrial Revolution began in the English textile industry. Textiles had been an important part of the English economy for centuries. On the eve of the Industrial Revolution, England's fine wools were famous. Linen production was expanding into Ireland and Scotland. Only the cotton industry was small and backward, unable to compete with Indian calico and muslin on either quality or price.

Weaving was a domestic industry in the first half of the eighteenth century. Except in Manchester, where self-employed weaver-artisans belonged to highly organized trade societies, most weavers were also farmers. In many households weaving was done in the seasons when there was little work to do on the farm. Often the entire family was involved.

The first changes were small:

- John Kay's flying shuttle, introduced in the 1730s and widely adopted in the 1750s and 1760s, allowed the weaver to speed up.
- Lewis Paul's carding machine, patented in 1748, made it easier to prepare fibers for spinning.

Both inventions intensified a supply problem that already existed: Spinners were the bottleneck in the system. It took three or four spinners to supply yarn for one weaver working a traditional loom. When the flying shuttle allowed a weaver to speed up, the yarn shortage became acute.

James Hargreaves's spinning jenny, patented in 1770, solved the yarn supply problem. Family spinning wheels were quickly replaced by small jennies, which were relatively cheap to buy and simple enough for a child to operate. In its earliest form the jenny had eight spindles. By 1784 eighty spindles were common. By the end of the century the largest jennies allowed one man, helped by several children, to operate as many as 120 spindles at once.

As spinning jennies grew bigger, spinning began to be moved into factories, but the new factory system did not replace the cottage-based textile industry immediately. At first families built extensions onto their cottages, where they could operate looms and jennies on a larger scale. Mill owners provided home-based spinners with raw cotton and handloom weavers with spun yarn. Because weavers could count on uninterrupted supplies of yarn, they could afford to weave full time instead of as a supplement to farming.

THE BIRTH OF THE FACTORY SYSTEM

The real change in the English weaving industry began in 1769, when Richard Arkwright patented the water frame, which improved both the speed and quality of thread spinning. Unlike the jenny, Arkwright's water-powered spinning frame was designed to be a factory machine.

A few years later Samuel Crompton's mule combined the principles of the jenny and the water frame, producing a smoother, finer yarn that allowed English cotton to compete with Indian goods in terms of quality. In 1795 Arkwright's patent was canceled, making the water frame available without restrictions for anyone who could afford the capital investment. That same year a steam engine was used to operate a spinning mill for the first time. Large-scale factory production was now feasible.

Improvements in spinning technologies were followed by carding, scutching, and roving machines that replaced the tedious hand labor of preparing fibers for spinning. Each technical improvement moved the textile industry further away from the domestic system.

The factory system was more than just a new way to organize work; it was a new way of life. Factories were dark, loud, and dangerous. The discipline and monotonous routine of the mill worker differed greatly from the workday of the farmer or hand weaver. Both agricultural workers and weavers often worked fourteen-hour days, but agricultural work was varied and seasonal, and independent weavers controlled their own schedules. In the factories the same fourteen hours included few breaks plus a long walk to and from home at the end of each day. Supervisors discouraged workers from song and chatter—both of which were hard to hear over the noise. As more women and children were hired, the fathers of families were thrown permanently out of work.

Child Labor Laws

The Parliament of the United Kingdom passed the first child labor law in 1802. Aimed at "apprenticeship" of orphans in cotton mills, it had no enforcement provisions—and little effect. The use of child labor was largely unchecked until the Factory Act of 1833, which set the legal work age at nine and stipulated that children between nine and thirteen could work no more than nine hours a day.

THE GROWTH OF FACTORY TOWNS

A New Landscape

As long as the new spinning mills were powered by water, they were scattered throughout northern England, located wherever falling water was available. Many of these mills were in places so isolated that their owners had trouble attracting enough labor, so they employed groups of children from London orphanages as "apprentices." With the introduction of steam power, it was possible to locate mills anywhere. Most were built near sources of coal and labor.

The key industrial cities grew at an astonishing rate in the first half of the nineteenth century, fueled by the internal migration of displaced workers, artisans, and shopkeepers in search of opportunities. The most rapid growth occurred in factory cities, like Manchester, Liverpool, and Birmingham, but port cities also grew as a result of expanded overseas trade. By 1850 more than half the British population lived in cities.

"Dark Satanic Mills"

The new cities were ugly to the nineteenth-century eye: hastily built and dark with the soot from burning coal. Contemporary observers were appalled by the impact of what poet William Blake described as the "dark Satanic mills" on the physical landscape. Critic John Ruskin foresaw an England "set as thick with chimneys as the masts stand in the docks of Liverpool: that there shall be no meadows in it; no trees; no gardens." Socialist artist William Morris feared that all would "end in a counting-house on the top of a cinder-heap...[where] the pleasure of the eyes was gone from the world." It took a foreigner, that keen-eyed observer Alexis de Tocqueville, to equate the physical ugliness of the mill towns with their effect on the people who worked in them: "From this foul drain the greatest stream of human industry flows out to fertilise the whole world," he wrote after a visit to Manchester. "From this filthy sewer pure gold flows. Here humanity attains its most complete development and its most brutish; here civilisation works its miracles, and civilised man is turned back almost into a savage."

THE POWER LOOM AND THE DECLINE OF WAGES

Weavers' wages, already driven down by the increase in weavers, took another hit when power looms were introduced on a large scale in the 1820s. Handlooms required skill to operate. Power looms did not.

The Luddites

In 1811 and 1812 masked bands of displaced textile workers attacked mills and destroyed the machines that were threatening their livelihood, calling themselves Luddites, after a possibly mythical leader named Captain Ned Ludd. The bands were careful not to attack villagers or damage other property and often had tacit local support. The government responded by making machine breaking punishable by death.

Unskilled factory labor, mostly women and children, began to replace independent skilled weavers. Because there were few other jobs available, wages remained low even when the market for British textiles boomed. Between 1820 and 1845 the cotton industry's production quadrupled; the wages it paid remained unchanged.

A Second Wave of Industry

The industrialization of Britain's textile industry created a demand for tools, machines, and power that spurred the development of improvements in forging steel and mining coal. The original wooden machines were replaced with faster and more specialized machinery, built from metal by a nascent machine tool industry.

Steam engines provided reliable and continuous power. First used for hauling coal from mines, the new technology was adapted to other industries as well. Soon steam engines were used in grain mills, sugar refineries, and the great British Potteries. The need for improved transportation led to the expansion of the canal system and the later development of roads and railways.

THE CREATION OF THE URBAN WORKING CLASS

The Industrial Revolution created a new class of urban poor as populations shifted from the countryside to the cities. The first generation that moved to the city often retained their rural roots, returning to their villages at harvest or for family celebrations. Over time ties to ancestral villages broke, and city dwellers saw themselves as substantially different from those who remained behind in the villages.

The transition from the countryside to the city was often difficult. Living conditions in the cities were horrific for the poor. Cities were unable to handle the influx of new residents. Sewers were open in working-class districts, and water supplies were inadequate. Older cities paved the streets in the mid-eighteenth century, but in new cities the streets were often no better than rutted paths. Existing housing was divided and re-divided to create space; families often had only one room or shared a room with another family. New housing was equally cramped and often badly built.

Small Business Owners

The Industrial Revolution also created a new class of wealthy manufacturers. A few were weavers and spinners who worked their way up from artisans to mill owners. Most started as small landowners or businessmen. They were a volatile element in a changing society: sometimes competing with wealthy landowners for power and status, sometimes joining with them to fight social change.

THE RISE OF WORKING-CLASS RADICALISM

The working classes did not wait for middle-class reformers to come to their rescue. Instead, they began to call for reform at the end of the eighteenth century: appealing to Parliament for minimum wage laws, apprenticeship regulations, child labor laws, and other protections for laborers; forming early versions of trade unions; and going on strike.

They soon came to the conclusion that the only way to effect real change was to reform the method of electing representatives to the House of Commons. As long as the landed classes (landowners who lived on rental income or on the produce from their land) controlled both houses of Parliament, there was no hope for reform.

Working-class radicals formed organizations called corresponding societies, which were designed to allow reformers from all over the country to stay in touch with each other. The most famous of these was the London Corresponding Society, formed in 1792 by radical shoemaker Thomas Hardy. Similar societies existed in industrial towns throughout Great Britain. As long as the corresponding societies remained local, the government left them alone. In 1793 a Scottish reform group attempted to bring representatives of many reform organizations to a meeting in Scotland. The leaders were arrested, tried for sedition, and sentenced to fourteen years' transportation overseas to one of Britain's penal colonies. A second attempt to organize a national reform meeting led to charges of high treason.

Reactions to the French Revolution

The French Revolution brought the march toward reform to a halt. Alarmed by the French example, and the enthusiasm with which it was greeted by some British radicals, the landed classes and manufacturers joined together against the radicals. Existing legislation related to apprenticeship, wage regulation, and conditions in industry were repealed. Existing laws against conspiracy were re-enforced by the Combination Acts of 1799 and 1800, which made it illegal for workingmen to "combine" to ask for higher wages or shorter work hours, or to incite other men to leave work.

PEACE AND POVERTY

England suffered a severe depression at the end of the Napoleonic Wars as a result of the transition to a peacetime economy. The sudden drop in government spending and the loss of wartime markets for British grain and manufactured goods brought with them falling prices, unstable currency, and widespread unemployment.

Dominated by landowners in both the House of Lords and the House of Commons, Parliament passed protective tariffs on grain as a way of solving the country's economic woes. The new Corn Laws protected landowners' incomes but forced urban laborers to pay a higher price for bread when times were already hard.

Workers reacted with strikes and bread riots across England. Moderate and radical reformers called for the repeal of the Corn Laws and for parliamentary reform in large public meetings. In 1817 the government attempted to defang the reform societies by temporarily forbidding all public meetings, suppressing all societies not licensed by the government, and suspending the Habeas Corpus Act, so that prisoners could be held without trial.

These severe measures brought only a temporary lull in popular demonstrations. In 1819 Britain's economic problems worsened. Reformers once again held mass meetings in the larger industrial cities. The most famous of these became known as the Peterloo Massacre. In August 1819 sixty thousand men, women, and children gathered on St. Peter's Field in Manchester to hear radical orator Henry Hunt speak. Fearful that a large group of reformers would turn into a large group of rioters, the local magistrate ordered a squadron of cavalry into the peaceful crowd to arrest Hunt. Eleven people were killed and several hundred were injured.

The government moved quickly to deter future demonstrations. Hunt and eight other organizers of the Manchester meeting were arrested and charged with holding "an unlawful and seditious assembling [sic] for the purpose of exciting discontent." Parliament passed the Six Acts: a series of drastic restrictions intended to eliminate unauthorized public meetings, suppress the radical press, and make it easier to convict popular leaders.

The Working-Class Movement Takes Another Path

The radical movement subsided after 1820, thanks to increased government repression and an economic upturn. For the next decade the working-class movement focused less on reform and more on building cooperative institutions: trade unions, friendly societies, mutual aid societies, and Working Men's Clubs. By 1832, when Parliament passed the Great Reform Act that gave the vote to much of the middle class, strong, self-consciously working-class institutions were in place to take up the battle.

THE INDUSTRIAL REVOLUTION IN CONTINENTAL EUROPE

At first the Industrial Revolution was a British phenomenon. Britain was determined to hold on to its manufacturing lead and made it illegal to export machinery and manufacturing technology. Skilled workers were not allowed to emigrate. It took a full generation for the Industrial Revolution to spread from Great Britain to other countries, such as Belgium, France, and the United States.

Other European powers lagged even further behind. Some parts of Germany, for example, did not begin industrial expansion until unification in 1871.

FOURIER, SAINT-SIMON, AND UTOPIAN SOCIALISM

The Moral Case

For many in France and abroad, the French Revolution followed the American Revolution in promising a brighter future for the lower classes, who had been trampled by the aristocracy. However, the egalitarian dreams, and nightmares, of the French Revolution did not last. Elements within the new French regime launched a Reign of Terror against actual and perceived enemies of the revolution. Thousands met their fate on the guillotine, a newly invented device for beheading. Gradually the regime began to devour itself. By 1795 the leaders of the revolution (termed the Directory) had turned conservative and did not welcome dissent against their rule. In 1799 they yielded the state to a military figure: Napoleon Bonaparte (1769–1821).

Bonaparte ruled France with greater and greater arbitrariness, and in 1804 he crowned himself emperor of France. This would have been concerning enough to other European powers, but the new emperor showed he was intent on expanding France's power and territories. For the next decade Europe was wracked by the Napoleonic Wars. They ended, finally, in 1815 with Napoleon's defeat by a coalition of nations on the field of Waterloo in Belgium. Napoleon was sent into distant exile, and the rest of Europe breathed a sigh of relief. Louis XVIII, fat and unimaginative, was placed on the throne as a puppet king.

However, a series of revolutionary uprisings against the king and his successors left France in a state of permanent instability. And against this background two of the most influential utopian social-ists put forth their ideas of social reorganization.

HENRI DE SAINT-SIMON AND THE SCIENTIFIC ELITE

Henri de Saint-Simon (1760–1825) was a French aristocrat whose family claimed descent from the first Holy Roman Emperor, Char-lemagne. Brought up to believe that he was destined for great things, Saint-Simon spent his early years in search of the next big idea. He fought on the side of the colonies in the American Revolution, win-ning the Order of Cincinnatus. At the end of the war he traveled to Mexico, where he tried to convince the Spanish viceroy to build a transoceanic canal through Lake Nicaragua. He became involved in an unsuccessful Dutch plot to drive the British out of India, then traveled to Spain with a plan for linking Madrid to the sea via canal.

Back in France he flung himself into the Revolution. He renounced his title, refused the office of mayor in his hometown in favor of a non-aristocratic candidate, ran revolutionary meetings, captained the local unit of the National Guard, and successfully speculated in real estate that the government seized from the Catholic Church.

In 1793 Saint-Simon was arrested as a result of a mistaken iden-tity. While in prison, he had a vision. Charlemagne appeared and told him that it was his destiny to be as great a philosopher as Char-lemagne was a warrior.

Once out of jail, Saint-Simon set out to turn himself into a great thinker. When his self-designed education was at an end, he began to write. He published his books himself and sent them to influential

SOCIALISM 101

thinkers of the day, hoping to interest them in his views. When he ran out of money, he took a clerical job and relied on the kindness of a former servant for his room and board. He copied his books by hand when he could no longer afford to have them printed.

Saint-Simon Diagnoses Society's Problems

While much early socialist thought was a reaction against the miseries caused by the Industrial Revolution, Saint-Simon embraced science and industry as the keys to human progress. He believed that the laws of social development could be discovered by studying history. He came to the conclusion that history alternates between periods of equilibrium and imbalance. Societies change as a result of struggle between the productive and unproductive classes: slaves and masters, serfs and lords, plebeians and patricians. The Middle Ages was a period of equilibrium, followed by the social disruption of the Reformation and the Revolution. Now society was poised for another period of equilibrium based on science and industry. The only thing that stood in the way was the semi-feudal power relationships that persisted in French society.

Unlike other socialist thinkers, Saint-Simon did not describe class struggle in terms of haves and have-nots. For him the conflict was between the productive classes and the parasites. Saint-Simon identified the vast majority of society in his own time as part of the productive "industrial/scientific" class, in which he included both workers and factory owners. Only the nobility and the clergy, who represented the last vestiges of feudal privilege, were unproductive. As long as the unproductive classes remained in power, they were a barrier to economic and social progress. For society to change, the modern productive classes had to recognize their common interests and band together.

Rule by the Scientific Elite

In his vision of the ideal society, Saint-Simon was still going for the big idea. Unlike other utopian socialists, who based their transformation of society on small groups, Saint-Simon envisioned a universal association that would incorporate the developed world. He wanted to organize society for the benefit of the poor, but he distrusted democracy. Instead, he proposed a cooperative commonwealth in which scientists, leaders of industry, and artists would replace the aristocracy and the military as the rulers of society.

"From Each According to His Ability..."

Saint-Simon wrote the famous dictum "from each according to his ability, to each according to his needs" to describe the distribution of wealth in his proposed society. Often attributed to Karl Marx, the phrase later became one of the distinguishing marks between socialism and communism.

Saint-Simon divided mankind into three classes: the savants, the propertied, and the unpropertied. The savants, including artists of all kinds as well as scholars, would be responsible for the moral and spiritual well-being of society, the role formerly held by the church. Actual governing and administration would be done by the propertied classes, specifically the captains of industry. The primary goal of society would be the material and intellectual improvement of the unpropertied, who would remain at the bottom of society until their own talents allowed them to rise.

Late in his life Saint-Simon decided his perfect society needed an ethical component. His first suggestion was a scientific religion. He later turned to what he called the New Christianity.

SOCIALISM 101

FOURIERISM

Charles Fourier (1772–1837) was the son of a cloth merchant. He lost his inheritance during the French Revolution and narrowly escaped the guillotine when the revolutionary troops besieged Lyon. During his career as a traveling salesman in the silk industry he saw first-hand the misery suffered by the silk workers in the first steps toward the Industrial Revolution.

Phalanx

The original meaning of *phalanx* was an infantry formation developed by Philip II of Macedonia, in which soldiers stood in close order with shields touching and spears overlapping. In the seventeenth century the word came to mean "any small, closely knit group of people." Fourier combined the word *phalanx* with *monastery* to get *phalanstery*.

Fourier did not believe social or economic inequalities were the source of human misery. Instead, he thought that most problems were the result of the society's misuse of people's "passions." Everyone has something they like to do. Every passion is good for something. If each passion could be put to its proper use, the "reign of Harmony" would prevail.

Fourier proposed the establishment of small communes, called phalanxes or phalansteries, which would allow society to make the best use of all human passions. Based on the number of personality types he believed existed, Fourier calculated that the optimum size of each phalanx would be about 1,600 people, a number that would get all necessary work done by assigning every passion to its proper job. (For instance, since small boys love dirt, they would have the job of disposing of the community's garbage.)

Despite the communal nature of the phalanxes, Fourier did not propose to abolish private property. Instead, each phalanx would be organized as a joint-stock company, in which individuals could invest. Everyone in the phalanx would be guaranteed a minimum subsistence and would have the opportunity to become an investor. Beyond their minimum subsistence, members would be paid based on the worth of their contribution to the community. Unpleasant work would pay a higher rate than work that was pleasant but useful. Useful work would pay more than work that produced luxuries. Any profits that the phalanx made would be distributed based on relative value, with five-twelfths going to labor, four-twelfths to capital, and three-twelfths to talent.

Brook Farm

The most famous Fourierist phalanstery was Brook Farm, which was founded outside of Boston in 1841 by a circle of transcendentalist ministers, reformers, and writers, including Nathaniel Hawthorne, Margaret Fuller, and the Alcott Family, including Bronson and Louisa May Alcott. Hawthorne wrote a novel based on the experience, *The Blithedale Romance* (1852).

Fourierism in Practice

After Fourier's death his ideas found two champions who did a better job of promoting Harmonism than Fourier ever did: Victor-Prosper Considérant and Albert Brisbane. Considérant established a single phalanx in France, which failed, and a second in Texas, *La Reunion*, which flourished for several years.

Brisbane was more successful. He brought Fourierism to the United States from France in 1840. With the help of Horace Greeley, founder and editor of the *New York Tribune*, Brisbane was able to introduce Fourier's theories to thousands of households across the northern states. His articles inspired the creation of more than forty phalansteries in the United States. Many of the communities combined Fourierism with transcendentalism, Swedenborgianism, perfectionism, or Spiritualism. Most lasted only a few years. The longest-lived of the Fourierist communities was the North American Phalanx, which existed from 1843 to 1855.

Horace Greeley

Horace Greeley (1811–1872) was the opinionated founder and editor of the *New York Tribune*. He supported a wide and eclectic range of causes, on and off the page, including free public schools, producer cooperatives, free speech, the emancipation of slaves, civil rights for freedmen, and westward expansion.

MARX AND SCIENTIFIC SOCIALISM

The Basics

Together, Karl Marx and Friedrich Engels produced the most significant theory in the history of socialism. They were the first socialist thinkers to present the possibility of a socialist state as a realizable goal rather than a utopian dream. Instead of creating a detailed prescription for a future society, they used the disciplines of German philosophy, French political thought, and English economics to understand how capitalism works. They came to the conclusion that the fall of capitalism would result from its internal contradictions.

THE "ODD COUPLE" OF SOCIALISM

From 1844 to Marx's death in 1883, Marx and Engels were political and intellectual collaborators. By Engels's own account, Marx was the originator and Engels was the popularizer. Engels always played second fiddle and was "happy to have had such a wonderful first violin as Marx."

It was an enormously productive and unlikely partnership. The two men came from very different backgrounds and had very different personal styles. Engels was well organized, well dressed, and charming. Marx was sloppy, careless about his appearance, often surly, and given to feuds with former associates. Marx wrote about social changes in terms of abstract social developments; Engels created detailed and compassionate pictures of how the working class lived.

KARL MARX

Karl Marx (1818–1883) was born into a middle-class Jewish family in the city of Trier, on the border between Germany and France. Both of Marx's parents came from distinguished rabbinical families.

University Years

Marx spent a year at the University of Bonn, where he indulged in the typical beer-swilling and saber-rattling behavior of a German university student of the time. He was soon in trouble with the university authorities for drunkenness and riotous behavior and with the police for subversive ideas. In the fall of 1836, with his father's wholehearted approval, he transferred from the party-school atmosphere of Bonn to the more serious University of Berlin. In order to please his father, Marx officially studied the law, but he soon neglected it in favor of the hottest subject of the day: philosophy. For a time he became a member of a group of German intellectuals who called themselves the "Young Hegelians" after the philosopher Georg Wilhelm Friedrich Hegel (1770–1831). When he graduated in 1841 with a doctorate in philosophy, Marx was considered the ablest philosophy scholar of his generation.

Old and Young Hegelians

After Georg Hegel's death in 1831, his followers split into two groups. The "Old Hegelians" defended his conservative belief that Prussia represented the apogee of historical development. The "Young Hegelians" used the revolutionary possibilities of Hegel's dialectic to critique religion, state, and society.

Marx As Editor, Husband, and Socialist Thinker

Denied an academic job because of his political views, Marx moved to Cologne, the center of the industrialized Rhineland, where he became the editor of the liberal newspaper the *Rheinische Zeitung*. At the newspaper he was exposed to problems for which Hegel provided no solutions, beginning with the debate over a bill designed to abolish the centuries-old communal privilege of picking up fallen wood in the forest. Marx had a new task: applying German philosophical thought to the realities of contemporary Germany.

When the government censor closed the *Rheinische Zeitung* in 1843, Marx accepted an offer to edit another radical paper, the *Deutsch-Französische Jahrbücher*, and moved to Paris with his new wife.

In the 1840s Paris was the center of both revolutionary politics and socialist thought. Marx met a number of critical socialist thinkers there, many of whom he would later quarrel with. He also began two new scholarly projects: a historical account of the French Revolution and an extended critique of Hegel's philosophy of law and the state. By the end of 1843 he had combined Hegel's dialectic with the historical model of the French Revolution to create a new concept of history as a process of transformation fueled by the struggle between two classes. In a capitalist society the wage-dependent proletariat would be the catalyst for change.

Marx didn't stay in Paris for long. In 1844 the Prussian government issued a warrant for his arrest as well as for other editors of the radical paper. Expelled from Paris, the Marx family moved to Brussels, where they lived until 1848.

FRIEDRICH ENGELS

Unlike Marx, Friedrich Engels (1820–1895) had personal experience with both capitalism and the effects of industrialization on the lives of the working class. The son and grandson of successful German textile manufacturers, Engels was born in the industrial town of Barmen, home to the first spinning machines in Germany. Friedrich Sr. was determined that his son would learn the textile business and join the family firm.

Furthering His Education

In 1838 Friedrich Sr. pulled Engels out of school and sent him to Bremen to work as a clerk in an export office, the nineteenth-century equivalent of getting an MBA. Away from his father's Protestant fundamentalism, Engels spread his wings and set out to educate himself. He read voraciously: philosophy, history, science, and the novels that were a forbidden frivolity at home. He wrote poetry, wrote theater and opera reviews, and did travel sketches. He joined a singing society, composed some music, and attended concerts by Franz Liszt. He also visited a ship that was sailing for America and was appalled by the difference between the first-class cabin and steerage. The first-class cabin was "elegant and comfortably furnished, like an aristocratic salon, in mahogany ornamented with gold." In steerage people were "packed in like the paving-stones in the streets."

In 1841 Engels left Bremen to complete his year of military service in Berlin. Still eager to educate himself, he chose Berlin because he hoped to attend lectures at the university while fulfilling his service requirements. Like Marx before him, he soon fell in with the Young Hegelians. He also met Moses Hess, who convinced him that communism was the logical outcome of the Hegelian dialectic.

Manchester, England

The following year Engels was sent to Manchester, where his father had a financial interest in a large textile factory. He worked in the factory as a clerk for almost two years, but he devoted his evenings to his own interests. Shocked by the conditions under which the English working classes lived and worked, he began to explore the city. He soon became involved with a young Irishwoman who worked in the Ermen & Engels factory, Mary Burns. (They married two years later.) With her sister, Mary became his guide to the parts of the city that a German manufacturer's son would never have found on his own. Together, they met with trade unionists, socialists, and other radicals. In what was left of his days he studied the English political economists, including David Ricardo.

Engels used the material he gathered to write two articles on social and economic conditions in Manchester that appeared in Marx's *Deutsch-Französische Jahrbücher*. (He later returned to the subject in his classic study of urban conditions during the Industrial Revolution, *The Condition of the Working Class in England*.) The articles included an early version of the Marxist critique of classical economics that stands at the heart of *Capital*.

Classical Economics

Karl Marx dubbed the British school of political economics that began with Adam Smith and reached its maturity in the writing of David Ricardo and John Stuart Mill "classical economics." Marx's critique of capitalism builds on their ideas about economic growth, free trade, and the labor theory of value, and uses many of the same model-building tools.

A Friendship with Marx

On his way home to Barmen in 1844 Engels stopped in Paris to see Marx, whom he had met earlier in Cologne. The brief stop stretched into ten days of continuous conversation. Engels later wrote, "When I visited Marx in Paris in the summer of 1844 we found ourselves in complete agreement on questions of theory and our collaboration began at that time."

DIALECTICAL MATERIALISM

The Philosophy of Scientific Socialism

Marx and Engels had been intellectually moving in the same direction before they met one another in 1844. Their first major collaboration was a series of essays later published as *Economic and Philosophic Manuscripts of 1844*. Both were greatly influenced in their philosophic approach by the philosophy of Georg Hegel.

Hegelian philosophy was the dominant philosophical system in Germany in the 1830s and 1840s. The central idea in Hegelian thought is the dialectic, which is often summed up in three words: *thesis, antithesis, synthesis*. Put simply, the conflict between two opposing views (thesis and antithesis) results in change (synthesis). The dialectic is a dynamic process: once a synthesis is produced, it becomes a thesis, which inevitably brings forth its own antithesis.

In his *Lectures on the Philosophy of World History* (1822–1823) Hegel applied the concept of the dialectic to the development of history, demonstrating how conflicting intellectual forces turn old societies into new ones. In his view history was the story of the progressive development of humanity from a state of savagery toward the ultimate goals of reason and freedom through the action of what Hegel called the "world spirit." The great men of history were those whose personal aims coincided with the dialectical movement of their times.

HISTORICAL MATERIALISM

Marx agreed with Hegel that history is a dialectical process and that change is consequently inevitable, but he didn't believe that the motive force for change was Hegel's abstract "world spirit." According to Marx, the history of civilization is the history of class conflicts, and the end result will be communism.

Marx identifies five stages of economic development in history: primitive communism, slavery, feudalism, capitalism, and socialism, which transitions into communism. In each of these stages, except for socialism/communism, there are inherent contradictions that make revolution inevitable. At some point in each stage of development the dominant mode of production (thesis) in a society comes into conflict with the society's existing relationships (antithesis), which are in themselves a product of the mode of production. What was once productive turns into shackles. Social revolution follows, creating a social system based on a different mode of production (synthesis).

This succession of conflicts will end with the arrival of socialism. Since there will no longer be private ownership of the means of production, there will no longer be the tension and contradictions of class divisions to fuel the dialectical movement of history. After capitalism falls there will be a period of transition to this new society, called the "dictatorship of the proletariat," followed by socialism, the first stage of communism.

THE REVOLUTIONS OF 1848

Europe Aflame

On January 12, 1848, the people of Palermo, Sicily, rose up against their ruler, Ferdinand II. It was the first of almost fifty revolutions that rocked Europe in the first four months of 1848. Armed rebellions occurred in France, Austria, Prussia, and most of the smaller German and Italian states. There was no single revolutionary organization or movement; no concerted effort across state lines. But the revolutions shared a strong resemblance as middle classes, proletariat, and peasantry united against absolutism and the remains of feudal privilege.

THE "HUNGRY FORTIES"

Economic conditions in Europe deteriorated throughout the 1840s. The widespread failure of grain crops created food shortages across Europe, made worse by the potato blight that lasted from 1845 to 1849. Grain prices increased by 100 to 150 percent over the course of two years, drastically affecting the standard of living for both peasants and workers in the cities, who typically spent 70 percent of their income on food. Food riots were common, escalating into violence directed at local landlords, tax collectors, and mill owners.

The crisis in agriculture was accompanied by industrial and financial collapse. Overproduction led to falling prices for manufactured goods, business failures among shopkeepers and wholesale merchants, and widespread unemployment. Bankrupt-cies and bank closings increased.

Irish Potato Famine

Ireland wasn't the only country hit by the potato blight in 1845, but it was the hardest hit. In the seventeenth century Oliver Cromwell's soldiers had pushed the native Irish into western Ireland. The land was too wet to grow grain, so they lived almost entirely on potatoes. When the crop failed in 1845, they had no food reserves.

Europe in Upheaval

A month after the revolt in Palermo the Paris mob overthrew Louis-Philippe's constitutional monarchy. The February Revolution in France triggered rebellions across Central Europe. In the German states uprisings appeared first in the Austrian Empire, then in many of the lesser German states, and finally in Prussia. At the same time revolutions spread through the Italian peninsula, from Palermo into Sardinia, Tuscany, the Papal States, and finally those parts of Italy that were under Austrian control.

Although the rebellions had their roots in the economic disasters of the "Hungry Forties," they quickly escalated into reaction against the suppression of liberalism, constitutionalism, and nationalism that marked European politics in the post–Napoleonic era. Social-ists flocked to the German states in particular to take part in what is sometimes described as the "revolution of the intellectuals."

Frightened monarchs learned from Louis-Philippe's mistakes and gave in to revolutionary demands for constitutions, representa-tive assemblies, and an expansion of personal freedoms. Only the unlucky Louis-Philippe lost his throne, though some of the more unpopular ministers were sent into exile.

By the end of April 1848 Tsar Nicholas I of Russia, writing to Queen Victoria, could say with only slight exaggeration, "What remains standing in Europe? Great Britain and Russia." For a brief time it appeared that the revolutionaries had won.

Areas the Revolution Missed

Tsar Nicholas wasn't entirely accurate in his assessment. Spain and the Scandinavian countries went untouched, while Great Britain suffered its own mild version of revolution in the form of a Chartist revival. The People's Charter, a six-point petition for many of the freedoms demanded by European revolutionaries in 1848, had been presented to Parliament unsuccessfully twice before, in 1838 and 1842.

THE FEBRUARY REVOLUTION IN FRANCE

In 1848 Louis-Philippe, the "citizen king" who took the throne following the revolution of 1830, still ruled France. The first years of his reign, known as the July Monarchy, were a clear victory of popular sovereignty over absolute monarchy. Social and political power shifted from the traditional aristocracy to the wealthy bourgeoisie, whom Louis-Philippe resembled in tastes and habits. Censorship was abolished and the National Guard restored. Catholicism was no longer the official religion. The voting age was reduced and the property qualification lowered, effectively doubling the electorate.

Nonetheless, there was plenty of warning that trouble was on the way. Food shortages, a rising cost of living, and widespread unemployment led to an increasing number of working-class demonstrations during the winter of 1847–1848.

In 1847, frustrated in their efforts to pass changes through normal legislative means and forbidden by law from holding political meetings, opposition leaders organized dinner parties to promote the cause of reform. Seventy banquets were held over the course of the winter, attended by members of the parliamentary opposition and republicans who accepted the institution of the constitutional monarchy. The campaign was scheduled to end with a bang: a procession followed by a large banquet on February 22 in Paris. The evening before the banquet, fearing violence, François Guizot's government banned both the dinner and the procession.

The Revolt

The following day, crowds of students and workers gathered in the streets. At first the police were able to disperse the crowds without difficulty. As the day went on, though, the crowds began to push back.

The revolt lasted only four days. At first Louis-Philippe refused to take the demonstrations seriously. On the second day members of the National Guard joined the demonstrators, and the crowd erected barricades in the streets. By the end of the day things had escalated too much for the king to ignore. He had two choices: bloodshed or appeasement. Louis-Philippe had seen the mob in action during the revolutions of 1789 and 1830. He chose appeasement and dismissed his chief minister. The gesture was a classic example of too little, too late. By February 24 things had gotten so bad in the capital that the king abdicated in favor of his nine-year-old grandson, the Count of Paris, and fled to England.

A New Government

With the revolutionaries in control of Paris and the king in flight, the Chamber of Deputies set aside an attempt by the king's daughter-in-law, the Duchesse d'Orléans, to have herself named regent for the Count of Paris. Instead, the Chamber selected a provisional government of moderate republicans for the newly born Second French Republic. At the same time the radical republicans chose their own provisional government. After more negotiations the two bodies reached a compromise and added three members of the radical faction to the moderate government, including socialist political philosopher Louis Blanc (1811–1882).

The Organization of Labor

Louis Blanc believed workers had a basic right to work and earn a decent living. He suggested the formation of "social workshops" as a step toward a fully cooperative society. His work *The Organization of Labor* (1839) influenced the demands of Paris laborers in the Revolutions of 1848.

Over the course of four months the division between the moderate and radical factions of the provisional government deepened. The moderates, supported by a majority of the French people, were primarily concerned with the questions of political reform that Louis-Philippe and his ministers refused to consider. The radicals, backed by working-class Paris, wanted social reforms, particularly improved conditions for workers.

The Right to Work

One of the primary demands of the Paris mob during the February Revolution was the right to work. Having helped to establish a new government, they expected it to provide work for everyone who wanted it.

The provisional government announced the establishment of "National Workshops" based on Blanc's proposal in *The Organization of Labor*. Blanc proposed autonomous cooperative workshops, controlled by the workers themselves, as the first step in a socialist transformation of society. Under the direction of the conservative minister of public works, Alexandre-François Vivien, the National Workshops became a relief project designed to keep the Paris mob from rising in revolt again. Enrollment in the National Workshops grew from 10,000 in March to roughly 120,000 in June. Many of the unemployed were put to work on road construction projects. Since there were more unemployed than there were roads to build, the surplus laborers were paid a small stipend.

National Elections

The split between Paris and the rest of France was demonstrated clearly on April 23, when the new republic went to the polls to elect representatives to the National Assembly, which would draw up the constitution. Out of nine hundred seats, five hundred went to moderate republicans and only one hundred to the radicals. To everyone's surprise the remaining three hundred seats went to avowed monarchists. Alarmed by radical threats to personal property, the peasants and the bourgeoisie had united against the radical republicans and the Paris proletariat.

June Days

The workers of Paris took to the streets once more on May 15. At first it looked like a repetition of the February Revolution. The crowd stormed the hall where the delegates were meeting, listened to speeches by the leaders of two of the revolutionary clubs, moved on to the Hôtel de Ville, and elected a provisional government.

Unlike Louis-Philippe, the newly elected executive committee of the Second Republic acted decisively. The National Guard cleared the assembly hall and reoccupied the Hôtel de Ville. Several of the leaders were jailed, and the revolutionary clubs were closed down.

On June 22, hoping to forestall further violence from the left, the government closed the National Workshops, which were essentially a proletarian army waiting for a leader. The decision backfired. Suddenly cut off from the payroll, thousands of workers took up arms.

The brief alliance between the workers and the lesser bourgeoisie was over. The assembly declared martial law in the capital and gave General Louis-Eugène Cavaignac full authority to bring the protest to an end. Cavaignac allowed the fighting to spread, then moved in with heavy artillery aimed at the barricades. At the end of three days an estimated 10,000 demonstrators were dead or wounded and 11,000 were taken prisoner. Cavaignac used his emergency powers to carry out vigorous reprisals against the suspected leaders of the insurrection. Most of the 11,000 prisoners were deported to Algeria.

REVOLUTION IN THE GERMAN STATES

Uprising in Marx's Homeland

The news of the successful revolution in France unleashed a series of smaller revolutions through the thirty-eight states of the German Confederation. As in France, the revolutionaries were a confused mixture of middle-class liberals looking for greater participation in government, urban workers and artisans angered by the effect of industrialization on their livelihood, and peasants rising up against inadequate land allotments and remnants of feudal dues and obligations. Most of the German rulers, willing to learn from Louis-Philippe's mistakes, promised to institute constitutions and other reforms before the revolutionaries even had a chance to organize.

The German Confederation

In 1815 the independent German states took the first step toward eventual unification. The German Confederation was a loose alliance formed for mutual defense. The Confederation had no central executive or judiciary. It also had no way to enforce cooperation among its members, an oversight that the two largest members of the Confederation, Prussia and Austria, used to their advantage.

THE FRANKFURT PARLIAMENT

In 1848 liberals from all over Germany made a concerted effort to unify the German states into a single political unit. The Frankfurt

Parliament was created by a group of middle-class German liberals who were inspired to action by the March revolts across Germany. They issued invitations to attend a preliminary parliament, which then arranged for delegates to a pan-German national parliament to be elected from all the German states.

Newspaper Editors

At the beginning of the uprising in Prussia Karl Marx and Friedrich Engels moved to the Prussian city of Cologne, where they founded and edited the liberal newspaper *Neue Rheinische Zeitung*. Because Marx had previously renounced Prussian citizenship, he was easily deported. Engels remained in Prussia and took an active part in the uprising.

The delegates met in the free city of Frankfurt for the first time on May 18, 1848. Journalists came from all over Europe for the opening ceremonies. Delegates and spectators believed they were witnessing the birth of a new nation, Germania. Once they settled down to work, the delegates discovered that while they agreed that their goal was a united German state, they disagreed on not only its form of government but also its boundaries. Supporters of "Little Germany" wanted a unified state that would include only Prussia and the smaller German states. Supporters of "Big Germany" wanted to add the German provinces of Austria.

The delegates had a further problem. The Frankfurt Parliament claimed to be a government speaking for the entire German people, but it was not recognized as such by the existing German governments or their princes. Misled by the temporary weakness of the Prussian and Austrian governments, besieged in their capitals by revolutionaries, the delegates assumed that the two states would follow the Parliament's lead and allow their states to be absorbed into a new German nation. They were wrong.

The new Austrian emperor, Franz Joseph I, made it clear that he had no intention of giving up the non-Germanic portions of his empire for the dubious privilege of being incorporated into the new German state. The delegates then offered the crown of "emperor of the Germans" to Friedrich Wilhelm IV of Prussia. At first Friedrich Wilhelm stalled. He couldn't accept the crown without the consent of the princes of the other German states. When twenty-eight of the princes agreed to accept the constitution under his rule, the Prussian king rejected what he called "a crown picked up from the gutter" and ordered the Prussian delegates to resign from the Parliament.

The Prussian delegates were soon followed by those from Austria and a number of the lesser states. The Frankfurt Parliament was reduced to its radical members, who tried to inspire the German people to continue the battle. Revolts occurred in a few of the lesser states in May 1849, but they were quickly suppressed, in many cases by Prussian troops.

REVOLUTION IN THE AUSTRIAN EMPIRE

The 1848 uprisings in the Austrian empire had a different character than those in Prussia and the lesser German states because Austria was not exactly a German state. The beginnings of industrialism in Vienna and other major cities created the usual patterns of social change, resulting in a growing bourgeoisie and a small urban proletariat. Peasants, who made up the overwhelming majority of the population, began to chafe against the demands of the *robota*, a type of forced labor owed to their landlords. But the real threat to the Austrian empire came from its multiethnic character.

The Habsburg dynasty of Austria ruled an empire that included ten different nationalities: Croats, Czechs, Germans, Hungarians, Italians, Poles, Romanians, Serbs, Slovaks, and Slovenes. In the 1840s these minority groups, most notably the Magyars of Hungary, began to have aspirations for national autonomy within the empire.

The Beginnings of a Revolt

The first responses to the news of the February Revolution in France were surprisingly mild. Students in Vienna sent a petition to the emperor requesting freedom of speech and the abolition of censorship. Hungarian nationalist Lajos Kossuth addressed the legislative body known as the Hungarian Diet, calling for an imperial constitution that would give virtual autonomy to Hungary. The students in Vienna quickly amended their petition to include a demand for a constitution.

On March 13 a clash between the army and a group of student demonstrators resulted in bloodshed. The emperor, Ferdinand I, called off the troops and announced his consent to the demands in the student petition.

Ferdinand's willingness to adopt moderate reforms did not answer the larger issue of ethnic autonomy. The emperor was soon on the defensive throughout the empire. The uprising in Vienna quickly spread to Prague, Venice, Milan, and Budapest. A war for liberation broke out in the empire's Italian possessions. In Budapest the Hungarian Diet adopted the decrees known as the March Laws, which created an independent Magyar state that was joined to the empire only through its allegiance to the emperor. Inspired by the Hungarian example, Czech nationalists in Prague demanded their own constitution and virtual autonomy. In June the first Pan-Slav Congress assembled in Prague and proposed that the Austrian empire be transformed into a federation of nationalities. (Pan-Slavism was a movement that proposed to establish links, formal and informal, between the various Slavic states of central and eastern Europe.)

Second and Third Uprisings

Back in Vienna Ferdinand reneged on his promise for a constitutional assembly and promulgated a constitution on his own. It was not liberal enough to satisfy the radical elements in the city. When the emperor then attempted to disband the National Guard and dissolve the radical student organization, Vienna suffered a second uprising by students, workers, and members of the National Guard. The imperial family was forced to flee the capital.

From May to October Vienna was in the hands of the revolutionaries, but the imperial army remained loyal to the Habsburg dynasty. While the emperor appeared to cooperate with the constituent assembly's efforts to draft a constitution, conservative statesmen and military leaders encouraged the military commander in Prague, General Alfred Windischgrätz, to drill his troops in preparation for recapturing the capital.

The Roots of War

Austria's failure to resolve the problems of a multiethnic empire ultimately led to the 1914 assassination of the Archduke Franz Ferdinand and his wife by a Serbian nationalist. The archduke's death triggered the tangled alliances that threw Europe into World War I.

A radical demonstration in Prague gave Windischgrätz an excuse to call for reinforcements and ruthlessly suppress the Czech revolutionary movement. When the general moved toward Budapest, Viennese radicals staged a third uprising. Windischgrätz used the violence as a pretext to bombard Vienna with artillery. The city was captured in early October, many radical leaders were executed, and the constituent assembly was exiled to Moravia.

With Vienna back in the government's hands, only the Hungarian revolt remained unchecked. Austria finally defeated the Hungarian rebels in August 1849, with help from Tsar Nicholas, who feared that Hungarian success might set off a similar revolt in Poland.

THE IMPACT OF THE 1848 REVOLUTIONS ON SOCIALISM

By 1849 the revolutions were over. Many radical revolutionaries felt they had gained nothing. The political situation in many countries was actually more repressive than it had been before the revolts. The constitutions that had been granted were suspended or watered down until they were worthless. Revolutionary leaders were imprisoned or exiled. The freedoms for which they had fought were systematically denied. With few exceptions, rulers still sat on the thrones they had occupied at the beginning of the uprising. France toppled the bourgeois monarchy of Louis-Philippe and voted for a new emperor in his place, Louis-Napoleon. The German states emerged from the upheavals with neither unity nor democracy. The ethnic minorities of the Austrian empire did not achieve their dreams of national autonomy. Italy was in fragments. French anarchist Pierre-Joseph

Proudhon summed up the feeling of many: "We have been beaten and humiliated...scattered, imprisoned, disarmed, and gagged. The fate of European democracy has slipped from our hands."

The defeat of the revolutions by reactionary forces changed the character of European socialism and the working-class movement. Before 1848 working-class radicals were often allied with the middle class against the traditional ruling classes. They fought together in many places at the beginning of the uprisings. As the revolutions progressed, the bourgeoisie aligned themselves with the old order, alarmed by the extremism of the mob and the perceived threat to private property.

MARX AND ENGELS WRITE A MANIFESTO

"A Spectre Is Haunting Europe"

In the mid-nineteenth century, as revolutions thundered about them, a good many socialist and communist organizations were struggling to make their voices heard. Most of them were tiny, but they loomed large in the minds of political commentators, who saw them as being at the heart of the current political unrest.

In 1847 two of these organizations merged: the League of the Just and the Communist Correspondence Committee. Together they formed the Communist League. To set out their principles they asked two of their members, Karl Marx and Friedrich Engels, to write a short introduction to socialist ideas. The result was *The Communist Manifesto*, one of the most famous political publications in history.

Socialism or Communism?

Is socialism the same thing as communism? It depends on whom you ask. Marxists generally agree that socialism and communism are two aspects of the same thing: a society based upon common ownership of the means of production. In his *The State and Revolution* Lenin identified socialism as the first stage of a progression toward communism. Under communism, Lenin argued, the state will "wither away" because there will be no need for it, given that all property will be owned in common.

The Communist Manifesto begins by pointing out the preoccupation of current political forces with communist ideas:

A spectre is haunting Europe—the spectre of communism. All the powers of old Europe have entered into a holy alliance to exorcise this spectre: Pope and Tsar, Metternich and Guizot, French Radicals and German police-spies.

Having hooked their audience, Marx and Engels offer their most basic explanation of their political and historical philosophy: "The history of all hitherto existing society is the history of class struggles."

From this starting point they review the rise of capitalism. Although Marx and Engels were unalterably opposed to it, they were quick to give capitalism its due: it had arisen from the innards of feudal society in the form of the urban merchant class. Gradually, through conflicts economic, political, and military, it had burst free of its origins and conquered and destroyed feudal social relationships. A class of serfs and peasants had been replaced by a class of workers, who sold their labor to the capitalists in return for wages. At the same time capitalism led to greater and greater productivity.

Just as capitalism grew within and transformed the feudal social system, so, argue Marx and Engels, the working class, the eventual destroyer of capitalism, was created by the capitalists themselves.

In the second half of the manifesto Marx and Engels put forward a practical course of action for the Communist League. They explain how it will work with other workers' political parties (it will cooperate with them but will speak to workers' broader interests) and offer some practical political demands, such as nationalizing railways, a progressive income tax, and free education.

At the end of forty impassioned yet logical pages Marx and Engels leave their readers with the famous call to action, "The workers have nothing to lose but their chains. They have a world to win. Workers of all lands, unite!"

The final version was published in London in February 1848—just before the outbreak of revolutions began in France. Several hundred copies were distributed to League members, but the organization never bothered to put it up for sale. By 1872 the *Manifesto* had been translated into Russian and French and issued in three editions in the United States and twelve in Germany.

Bourgeoisie and Proletariat

Marx and Engels, like virtually all of their socialist contemporaries, looked to the French Revolution for inspiration. As a result, they made use of certain French terms in their writing. They called the capitalist class the *bourgeoisie* and the working class the *proletariat*. Use of these terms continued throughout the socialist movement, in some cases up to the present day.

Most of what Marx and Engels (and many other socialist leaders) wrote was in answer to criticism or commenting on events. There is no book in which Marx says, "Okay, this is what I mean by socialism and how we get there!" *The Communist Manifesto* is as close as we're going to get, and as such it's an important starting point for understanding Marx.

MARX'S METHOD

The *Manifesto* is also a window into how Marx sees other socialists. He is critical of those such as Fourier and Saint-Simon; he dismisses them as "utopian socialists" in that they assume social change can be imposed on a society by well-intentioned members of the upper classes.

The document also offers a clear example of how Marx and Engels applied Hegel's dialectic to history. Hegel, if you remember, argued that each stage of an idea contains within it the seeds of its own destruction. Thus, the thesis contends with the antithesis, and in time the two are replaced by a new synthesis. Hegel believed that his philosophy applied only to ideas, but Marx applied it to history and politics.

Marx versus Feuerbach

Marx had begun to move in this direction several years earlier. In 1845 he and Engels wrote a series of short notes for a book later published as *The German Ideology*. The notes gained the name "Theses on Feuerbach" because they were a critique of the writings of the German philosopher Ludwig Feuerbach (1804–1872). Like Marx, Feuerbach was a disciple of Hegel, but Marx and Engels took things much further. In their eleventh thesis they wrote, "Philosophers have hitherto only *interpreted* the world; the point, however, is to *change* it."

Thus feudal society gave birth to a nascent capitalist class. That class grew in strength until it overthrew its parent and created what became the industrial working class. In turn the working class was destined, Marx and Engels argued in the *Manifesto*, to overthrow capitalism.

MARX AND ENGELS IN THE REVOLUTION OF 1848

Shortly after *The Communist Manifesto* was published, the compost hit the fan in France. With revolution in the air, the Belgian authorities decided that Marx was an undesirable alien and asked him to leave the country. As one door closed, another opened; Marx returned to France at the invitation of the new republican government.

Within weeks of the March uprising in Prussia, Marx and Engels were on their way to Cologne, Marx traveling on a temporary French passport because he had given up his Prussian citizenship several years before. (His application for British citizenship was denied because he gave up his Prussian citizenship.) Finally, he chose to take refuge in Great Britain. London was Marx's home for the rest of his life.

With Marx gone, Engels closed down the paper. He remained in Prussia, where he took an active part in the final stages of the uprising. As the revolution drew to a close, Engels escaped to Switzerland and then made his way back to England.

After the Revolution

By the end of 1849 the revolutions in Europe were over and Marx and Engels were both settled in England. Engels went back to work in his father's factory, first as a clerk and later as a partner. For the next twenty years he led a double life in Manchester: member of the business elite by day, revolutionary by night.

Marx and his family settled in London. He spent his working days in the British Museum reading room, where he wrote prolifically and educated himself in economics with the help of parliamentary blue books and Engels's firsthand experience of British industry. His only regular income came from writing articles on the European political situation for Horace Greeley's *New York Tribune* at the rate of £1 per article. He depended heavily on Engels, who often ghostwrote the *Tribune* articles and gave him money with a generous hand. It is one of history's ironies that the Engels family's factory in Manchester supported Marx as he studied and wrote about the downfall of capitalism.

CAPITAL

The Foundation of Marxism

During his years in exile in Britain Marx worked remorselessly on his theory of capitalism, seeking to explain how it worked and how it must inevitably succumb to the forces of history. In 1867 he published the first volume of his masterpiece, *Capital*. He described his purpose in writing the work as laying bare "the economic law of motion of modern society." In it, Marx examined the models of the classical economists in terms of his theory of class struggle. The result is an analysis of the economic injustices of the capitalist system and contradictions in the system that would create its ultimate fall.

Capital in Russia

The Imperial Russian censor approved a Russian translation of *Capital* for publication in 1872 on the grounds that "it is possible to state for certainty that very few people in Russia will read it and even fewer will understand it."

MARX'S CRITIQUE OF CAPITALISM

According to Marx, the class conflict that will bring an end to capitalism lies in the contradictory economic interests of the bourgeoisie and the proletariat, specifically in regard to the value of labor. The labor theory of value, as defined by David Ricardo, argues that the value of a product is determined by the amount of labor needed to produce it. Before capitalism, economies were based on the exchange of useful products. Under capitalism, products became commodities to be bought or sold for a profit. Labor has also become a commodity, but its price is not as great as the value of the product it creates. Marx called the difference "surplus value."

SURPLUS VALUE

Under capitalism, those who own the means of production, like factory owners, produce commodities for sale in the market in order to make a profit. To do so, they need two kinds of capital:

- Constant capital (e.g., raw material, machinery, and buildings), which does not change its value during production
- Variable capital (i.e., labor), which does change its value during production

Profit comes through the variable value of labor. The base value of a laborer is her wage. If she works for eight hours and produces enough goods to cover her wage in the first four hours of the day, everything that she produces in the second four hours is surplus value. Surplus value is the source of the capitalist's profits and her ability to invest in new machinery and technology.

Women's Work

Those feminine pronouns aren't an attempt at political correctness. Surplus value was an even bigger issue for women than men. In the 1830s and 1840s more than half of the factory workers and coal miners in Europe were women. Children of both sexes earned roughly the same wage. After the age of sixteen women earned roughly one-third of a man's wage.

The basic economic struggle between labor and capitalist was over what Marx called the "rate of surplus value" or, more negatively, the "rate of exploitation." Owners wanted to increase the rate through longer hours and/or lower wages. Labor wanted to decrease the rate through shorter hours and/or higher wages.

According to Marx, the struggle over the rate of surplus value revealed an inherent flaw in capitalism. In order to remain competitive, capitalists needed to modernize their machinery, which required them to increase their investment in constant capital at the expense of labor's share of the surplus value. More efficient production meant more commodities reached the market, but reduced wages meant laborers could not afford to buy more goods, causing a crisis of overproduction. At each crisis of overproduction stronger companies would force weaker competitors out of business. With fewer companies in business, unemployment would rise and wages would go down, causing more poverty among the proletariat. Lower wages meant the businesses that survived were able to keep a larger share of surplus value as profit. Eventually, the economy would recover as a result of the new capital that business owners accumulated, and the cycle would resume. Each crisis would be more serious than the last, leading to the eventual breakdown of capitalism and the rise of communism in its place.

Analysis of a Commodity

Although the scope of *Capital* is extremely broad, volume 1, chapter 1 starts with Marx's analysis of a single commodity. Thus, he establishes the basic form of his argument: a commodity's value is determined by the labor that went into creating it, and that *only* human labor can create value.

CLASS CONSCIOUSNESS

According to Marx, capitalist society is divided into two classes: those who control the means of production and those who sell their labor. Throughout history the relationship between classes has always been one of exploitation and domination: "Freeman and slave, patrician and plebeian, lord and serf, guild-master and journeyman, in a word, oppressor and oppressed stood in constant opposition to each other." As in the historical stages before it, the structure of capitalism created a natural antagonism between its two fundamental classes: bourgeoisie and proletariat. Class struggle would end with the destruction of capitalism, because communism would be a classless society.

ENGELS COMPLETES MARX'S WORK

Although Marx had compiled a vast amount of notes for the next two volumes of his work, he did not live to complete them. Worn out from work and living on the edge of poverty, Marx died on March 14, 1883. It was left to his comrade, Engels, to compile and edit the notes to create the final two volumes of the work.

Speaking at Marx's grave in 1883, Engels described Marx's place in history:

As Darwin discovered the law of evolution in organic nature, so Marx discovered the law of evolution in human history...that human beings must first of all eat, drink, shelter and clothe themselves before they can turn their attention to politics, science, art and religion.

Having spent the previous thirty-five years making sure that the Marx family members were, in fact, able to eat, drink, and shelter and clothe themselves, Engels devoted the rest of his life to editing and published the remaining two volumes of *Capital*. He also continued political work, eventually forming the organization known as the Second International, an association of socialist parties from around the world.

Marx's Daughters

Two of Marx's three daughters, Laura and Eleanor, also played significant roles in the socialist movement. Laura Marx Lafargue (1845–1911) translated her father's work into French. She and her husband, Paul Lafargue, were active in French socialist politics and also helped spread Marxism to Spain. Eleanor Marx Aveling (1855–1898) was one of the leaders of the British Social Democratic Federation and later the Socialist League. She worked in support of numerous strikes and other socialist activities. Like her sister, she was a translator, primarily of dramatists. She translated several works by the Norwegian playwright Henrik Ibsen into English.

CIVIL WAR IN FRANCE

The Paris Commune

In 1871 the Franco-Prussian War brought the Second Empire of France to a humiliating end. The newest version of the National Assembly was prepared to reestablish the monarchy, again. Angered by both events, the workers of Paris took to the streets in protest, seized command of the city, and founded their own short-lived government. Watching the rise and defeat of the Paris Commune from London, Marx described it as the first proletarian revolution. Later historians have suggested that it was the last convulsion of the French Revolution of 1789.

THE SECOND EMPIRE

Prior to the Revolution of 1848, Napoleon Bonaparte's nephew, Louis-Napoleon Bonaparte (1808–1873), tried to take the French throne by force twice. Each time the would-be king was stopped and sent into exile.

When the revolution broke out in 1871, Bonaparte hurried to Paris to place his claim again. The provisional government was no happier to see him than their predecessors had been in 1836 and 1840, but he was not entirely without supporters. When the time came, the small Bonapartist party nominated him for a seat in the National Assembly. He was elected deputy by Paris and three other districts but refused to take his seat because conditions were so unsettled. In September he was elected again, this time by five districts.

Bonaparte began to campaign for the presidency as soon as he arrived in Paris to take his place in the Assembly, evoking the glamour of the Napoleonic legend and indiscriminately promising to protect the interests of all voting groups. In December 1848 he was elected by an overwhelming majority to a four-year term as president of the Second Republic, the only candidate to receive votes from all classes of the population.

Bonaparte had no interest in being president. Instead, he had his eye on his uncle's old job as emperor. He spent his first year in office in a power struggle with members of the Assembly, most of whom favored a return to the Bourbon or Orléans monarchies. When the Assembly refused to revise the constitution to allow his reelection, Bonaparte staged a coup d'état on December 2, 1851. A year later he took the title of Emperor Napoleon III, an act that was also ratified by the voting public.

"Napoleon the Little"

France enthusiastically supported Napoleon III in the restoration of the empire, expecting a revival of Napoleonic glory. If they didn't get glory, at least they got comfort. Under Napoleon III's rule, France enjoyed two decades of domestic prosperity for the middle and upper classes. Surrounded by Saint-Simonian advisors, the emperor threw the state's resources at encouraging industrial development, resulting in increased industrialization, the creation of a national railroad system, imperial expansion in Asia and Africa, and Baron Haussmann's transformation of Paris into what author Rupert Christiansen called "a crazy tinsel circus of all fleshly pleasures and all earthly magnificence." The emperor even remembered to throw a bone to the working classes in the form of lower tariffs on food.

Not satisfied with domestic success, Napoleon III wanted to reestablish France's position as a powerful player in Europe. However, he damaged French relations with both Russia and Austria and helped replace weak neighbors with the powerful new states of Germany and Italy.

THE FRANCO-PRUSSIAN WAR

Looking at Napoleon III's foreign policy track record, one member of the National Assembly, Adolphe Thiers, concluded, "There are no mistakes left to commit." He was wrong. On July 19, 1870, the emperor crowned his diplomatic errors in Europe by declaring war on Prussia.

By July 30 the Prussian chancellor, Otto von Bismarck, had almost 500,000 men in the field, drawn from both the Prussian army and those of its allies among the smaller German states. The French mustered less than half that number, badly organized, badly equipped, and badly led by Napoleon III himself, who really wasn't the military leader that his uncle had been. The Germans soon had one French army bottled up at Metz, near the German border in Lorraine, and another cornered slightly to the west at Sedan. On September 1 the French were decisively beaten at the Battle of Sedan, and the Germans captured Napoleon III and a large portion of the French army.

The Siege of Paris

When the news reached Paris three days later, republican members of the Assembly proclaimed the establishment of a new republic and set up an emergency government of national defense. On September 19 German forces surrounded Paris.

For the first six weeks of the siege Paris enjoyed an almost festive mood. The city stayed in contact with the outside world through the use of hot-air balloons and carrier pigeons.

Resistance

Léon Gambetta, a Paris attorney and the new minister of war and the interior, escaped from the besieged capital in a hot-air balloon on October 7 and organized a resistance movement in the provinces. Under Gambetta's leadership, untrained and undersupplied guerilla forces successfully harassed the German supply lines but were unable to get a relief force through to Paris.

With the onset of cold weather, conditions grew harder and the festive mood evaporated. The winter of 1870 proved to be one of the coldest on record in the nineteenth century—so cold that the Seine froze solid for three weeks. The price of fuel quadrupled. Smallpox, typhoid, and pneumonia ran through the population. Communications with the world outside the city became less reliable when it became too cold for the pigeons to fly. More than 200,000 refugees poured into the city ahead of the German troops, only to find no housing or livelihood. Business ground to a halt, creating massive unemployment and leaving small middle-class businesses in ruins.

Worst of all, food supplies ran low. Early in the siege voices from the left, including socialist agitator Auguste Blanqui, argued for mandatory food rationing. Assuming in October that the siege would end quickly, the government chose to ration meat instead of grain and left the city to the vagaries of the free market.

Those who had money and foresight stockpiled food in the early days of the siege, but most scrambled to find food. Municipal authorities did what they could. The mayors in the city's working-class *arrondissements* (administrative districts) opened soup kitchens and employed women to sew uniforms for the National Guard.

Wealthy versus Poor

The threat of starvation did not affect everyone equally. The wealthy bought horsemeat and, when the Paris zoo could no longer feed its animals, elephant, kangaroo, and yak. Rat salami became a delicacy, and butchered cats were sold as "gutter rabbits." The average working-class family couldn't even afford to eat rat.

In early January the Germans upped the pressure by bombarding the city. Rumors spread that the government had stockpiles of food in the forts surrounding Paris. The number of radical political clubs in the city increased, spawning a resurgence of revolutionary socialism. Revolutionary organizations placarded the city with posters denouncing the government's handling of the war and demanding that it relinquish its authority to the people of Paris.

With Paris in a state of starvation, and no relief in sight from either Gambetta's guerillas or the other European powers, the provisional French government signed an armistice on January 28, 1871, deposing Napoleon III.

THE WORKERS' INSURRECTION

The citizens of Paris were not happy. They had experienced the burden of the war during the four-month siege of the city. They had watched the Germans march through the Arc de Triomph, a small humiliation provided for in the peace treaty. They resented the transfer of the government to Versailles rather than to Paris—a symbolic statement in favor of monarchy over republic.

In February the conservative majority in the Assembly passed three laws that did nothing to improve the negative attitude in Paris:

- They ended the wartime moratorium on debt repayment.
- They required the immediate payment of any rent that was not paid during the war.
- They canceled the pay of the National Guard, which was composed of workers who had defended Paris during the siege.

This last decision was intended to demobilize the National Guard, which significantly outnumbered the regular army units then at the government's disposal; it deprived many working-class families of their only income.

The National Guard took the first step of resistance, organizing itself into a governing federation under a central committee with the broad mandate of safeguarding the republic. Within a few days the Central Committee of the National Guard federation was the unofficial power. It made no moves toward violent revolution, but it took the precaution of securing the city's chief arsenals and seizing four hundred cannons that were left behind by the regular army.

Instead of trying to defuse the situation, the head of the government, Adolfe Thiers, sent six thousand regular army troops into the city early in the morning on March 18 to recapture the cannons from the working-class district of Montmartre and bring the city under control. Thiers's troops easily overran the Guard unit and recaptured the cannons. Only then did they realize that they had forgotten to bring horses to haul the cannons away. While the army scrambled for horses, an agitated crowd gathered. As usual, when the Parisian mob and the army interacted, things grew violent. Even though the soldiers refused orders to fire on their fellow citizens, two generals were captured and lynched by a mob that included army troops.

What started out as resistance against the effort to disarm the city turned into a full-scale insurrection. As violence spread through the city, Thiers withdrew all troops and government offices out of Paris to Versailles.

THE ELECTION OF THE COMMUNAL COUNCIL

On March 26 Parisians repudiated the authority of the National Assembly and elected their own government, calling it the Paris Commune after the revolutionary government of 1793. The leaders of the new government were a mixed group of old-style Jacobins, anti-clericals, miscellaneous socialists, and political opportunists. (During the French Revolution in the eighteenth century, the Jacobins represented the far left in the Assembly.)

The "First Dictatorship of the Proletariat"

The leaders of the Paris Commune seemed curiously unaware that controlling Paris was not the same thing as controlling France.

The Commune called for a decentralized government, the separation of church and state, and the replacement of the regular army by the citizen-controlled National Guard. None of these provisions could be carried out because the authority of the Commune was confined to Paris. The only practical legislation that was passed was a renewal of the wartime moratorium on rents and debts, the institution of a ten-hour workday, and the abolition of night work in bakeries, suggesting that at least one tired baker served in the Commune's legislature.

Other Communes

On March 22 the National Guard battalion at Lyon followed Paris's lead, seizing control of the town government and establishing a provincial commune. Similar uprisings occurred in Saint-Étienne, Marseille, Toulouse, Limoges, Narbonne, and Le Creusot, but they were quickly suppressed. By April 4 the Paris Commune stood alone against the government at Versailles.

"The Bloody Week"

While the leaders in Paris spent their time passing impractical legislation, Thiers built up the military strength of the government at Versailles. He was helped in his preparations by a successful appeal to Bismarck. Never a fan of revolution, Bismarck released a large number of French prisoners of war to help Thiers retake the capital.

Thiers's forces laid siege to Paris at the beginning of April. After several weeks of bombarding the city, government troops entered an undefended section of Paris on May 21. The street fighting over the course of what came to be called "the bloody week" was more brutal than anything in the recent war against the Germans. The Communards, as the supporters of the Commune were called, set up barricades and fought the army's advance street by street. In the last days of fighting, the Commune's soldiers, seeing that their cause was lost, shot their prisoners and hostages, including the archbishop of Paris, and set fire to the public buildings of the city. On March 28 the last organized defenders of the Commune made a final stand at the cemetery of Père-Lachaise, where, conveniently, they were executed by the National Assembly's troops. All over the city men suspected of having fought for the Commune were rounded up and shot without trial.

Approximately 20,000 Communards and 750 soldiers died during "the bloody week." Of the roughly 38,000 arrested, some 7,000 were deported to the penal colony of New Caledonia in Melanesia. Others escaped into exile.

THE END OF ONE REVOLUTION OR THE BEGINNING OF ANOTHER?

Socialist theorists of all types claimed the Paris Commune for themselves. On May 30, 1871, two days after the Paris Commune died in the cemetery of Père-Lachaise, Karl Marx read his report on the event to the General Council of the International Workingmen's Association, later published as a pamphlet titled *The Civil War in France*. Marx declared that the Commune was the "first dictatorship of the proletariat," notable less for its actual accomplishments than for its symbolism. Later revolutionaries used the example of the Commune for their own purposes, with varying degrees of historical accuracy. Both Vladimir Lenin and Leon Trotsky held up the demise of the Commune as an example of what happens when revolutionaries try to build bridges across class lines. The Soviet Union claimed the Commune as one of its illustrious ancestors.

The anarchist Peter Kropotkin summed up the appeal of the Paris Commune in the mythology of socialist revolution in his own pamphlet on the subject:

Why is the idea represented by the Commune of Paris so attractive to the workers of every land, of every nationality? The answer is easy. The revolution of 1871 was above all a popular one. It was made by the people themselves, it sprang spontaneously from the midst of the mass, and it was amongst the great masses of the people that it found its defenders, its heroes, its martyrs. It is just because it was so thoroughly "low" that the middle class can never forgive it. And at the same time its moving spirit was the idea of a Social Revolution; vague certainly, perhaps unconscious, but still the effort to obtain at last, after the struggle of many centuries, true freedom, true equality for all men. It was the Revolution of the lowest of the people marching forward to conquer their rights.

ANARCHISM VERSUS MARXISM

Bakunin and Marx

In the aftermath of the Paris Commune Marx and Engels confronted those whose political views they believed were in complete disagreement with their own. The Commune had been a practical working-out of socialist theory, despite its defeat. Marx and Engels realized that their political opponents included not only other socialists but anarchists as well. Thus, they confronted one of the great revolutionary figures of the nineteenth century, the theorist of anarchy, Mikhail Bakunin.

Mikhail Bakunin (1814–1876) was born into a conservative noble family in Russia. He served briefly in the Russian army on the Polish frontier before plunging into the intellectual life of Moscow and Premukhino, where he studied romantic Hegelianism and became friends with the novelist Ivan Turgenev.

In 1840 Bakunin traveled to Berlin. Like others before him, he fell in with that nursery school for revolutionaries, the Young Hegelians, who introduced him to another side of Hegel. After brief periods in Berlin and Switzerland he made his way to Paris. In Paris he met a number of Polish émigrés, who interested him in the possibilities of combining the struggle for national liberation with social revolution.

TRAVELS AND ESCAPES

Always more interested in action than in theory, Bakunin was deeply involved in the 1848 revolutions. He followed the uprisings from Paris to Prague to Dresden, traveling on false passports and always one step ahead of the police. The authorities caught up with him after the revolution in Dresden failed. He was arrested and condemned to death. The Dresden authorities happily handed him over to the Austrians, who had a warrant out for his arrest for his revolutionary activity in Prague. The Austrians condemned him to death again, carried him to the border, took back their handcuffs, and handed him over to the Russians.

After six years in the Peter and Paul Fortress in St. Petersburg, Bakunin was exiled to a Siberian prison that was run by one of his mother's cousins. In 1861 he escaped. Traveling on an American ship by way of Japan, San Francisco, and New York, he made his way to London, a haven of nineteenth-century European refugees from both the left and right.

For several years Bakunin batted around Europe, going anywhere there was a revolution in process. He slowly realized that revolutionaries who were fighting for national liberation usually had no interest in broader social change. Having come to the conclusion that social revolution must be international to succeed, he settled in Italy and began to create a complex network of secret societies—some real, some fictional—that he called the International Social Democratic Alliance.

ANARCHO-COMMUNISM

Bakunin adapted Pierre-Joseph Proudhon's teachings to create the doctrine later known as anarcho-communism. He shared Marx's vision of communism as a classless society but rejected the idea of a central state. Instead, he believed that land, natural resources, and the means of production should be held by local communities, which would form a loose federation with other communities for joint purposes.

Bakunin advocated the use of terror and violence as a weapon to destroy organized government, claiming that "the passion for destruction is also a creative urge." He argued that the state exists to protect private property, and private property protects the state. Therefore, the state must be destroyed before property can be communally owned and equally distributed. Paradoxically, the only way to create a free and peaceful society was through violent revolution.

Proletariat or Peasant?

Marx and Engels were convinced that the revolution would begin with the industrial working class in the most advanced capitalist societies, where the conflicts between capital and labor were most acute. Bakunin disagreed. He argued that revolutionary change was most likely in the least economically developed countries because their workers were less privileged. Bad as life was for a factory worker in Manchester, England, it was worse for workers in less developed countries. He made a strong argument that Russian peasants would lead the charge in the revolution. Not only were Russian serfs still legally tied to the land as late as the Emancipation Manifesto of 1861, but they also had traditional village communal structures that would form a great foundation for socialism.

THE FIRST INTERNATIONAL

In 1864 Marx drew up the founding statement for the International Workingmen's Association, later known as the First International.

Bakunin's supporters immediately challenged the idea of creating a formal organization to win support for communism, asking, "How can you expect an egalitarian and free society to emerge from an authoritarian organization?"

The battle between Marx and Bakunin over the control of the First International came to a head in 1872, when Marx and Engels engineered the expulsion of Bakunin and his followers from the First International.

Bakunin's Prediction

Bakunin accurately predicted the nature of Marxist dictatorships in the twentieth century: "The so-called people's state will be nothing other than the quite despotic administration of the masses by a new and very non-numerous aristocracy of real and supposed learned ones."

THE ANARCHIST PRINCE

Peter Kropotkin (1842–1921) was the son of a Russian prince. He was educated at an elite military school and served for several years as an officer in Siberia. He resigned his commission in 1867, studied mathematics in St. Petersburg, and became a professional geographer, specializing in the mountain ranges and glaciers of Asia.

In 1871 Kropotkin brought a promising scientific career to a halt. He turned down the secretaryship of the Russian Geographical Society, renounced the title of prince, and joined the revolutionary movement in St. Petersburg. For several years he worked as part of the Tchaikovsky Circle, which distributed revolutionary propaganda to Russian workers and peasants.

Arrested in St. Petersburg in 1874, Kropotkin began a variation of the experience of arrest, expulsion, and escape common to radical reformers of the period. He was held without trial but managed to escape from the prison hospital and make his way to Western Europe. Expelled from Switzerland at the demand of the Russian government in 1881 and arrested in France in 1883, he sought refuge in England, where he made his living as a respected scientific journalist.

Kropotkin was the most widely read of the anarchist theorists. Between 1883 and 1917, when he returned to Russia, he contributed articles on anarchism to leading liberal magazines, radical papers, and the eleventh edition of the *Encyclopædia Britannica*. His anarchistic journalism was translated and published worldwide. Several of his books were published as magazine serials.

Kropotkin tried to give anarchism a scientific basis. The most influential of his works was *Mutual Aid* (1902). In it, he refuted the popular theory of social Darwinism, which justified competition in a free-market economy in terms of survival of the fittest. He demonstrated from observation of both animal and human societies that competition within a species is less important than cooperation as a condition for survival.

The Propaganda of the Deed

In the 1870s French and Italian anarchists began to use a phrase that would become one of the most visible and controversial anarchist doctrines: *the propaganda of the deed*. The idea was that violent action is the most effective form of propaganda for the revolutionary cause.

At first the propaganda of the deed referred to rural insurrections intended to rouse the Italian peasantry to revolt. Later, the doctrine became the justification for assassinations and bombings of public places carried out by individual protesters. Sometimes working alone, sometimes as part of a conspiracy, anarchists carried out a series of attacks on prominent political figures, beginning with the attempt to assassinate Kaiser Wilhelm I in 1878.

Assassinations Spread

Assassinations of prominent political figures became more common with the ready availability of dynamite, which some revolutionaries welcomed as the "artillery of the proletariat." Patented by Alfred Nobel in 1867, the explosive was widely manufactured by 1875. One anarchist, Johann Most, gave instructions for whipping up a batch at home in *The Science of Revolutionary Warfare* (1885).

Important figures in the anarchist movement repudiated the technique as fundamentally useless. As Kropotkin put it, "A structure based on centuries of history cannot be destroyed with a few kilos of dynamite." Such protests were useless; the lone bomber became the public image of anarchy.

THE RISE OF SOCIAL DEMOCRACY

Socialism Becomes a Mass Movement

In the 1860s Europe was beginning to recover from the first traumas of the Industrial Revolution. There was no sign that Marx's proletariat revolution was imminent. Capitalism was flourishing. Economic and political injustices remained, but governments began to enact labor laws, lift restrictions on trade unionism, and open the political process, largely as a result of pressure from the socialist and labor movements. Some German socialists began to reconsider the inevitability of the Marxist revolution and look toward the possibility of political action.

WHAT IS SOCIAL DEMOCRACY?

During the late nineteenth and the early twentieth centuries a wide range of socialists adopted the term *social democrat* to distinguish themselves from socialists who advocated violent revolution. The basic tenet of social democracy is the belief that socialist reforms can be achieved democratically through the election of socialist representatives. Social democrats advocate a peaceful, evolutionary transition from capitalism to socialism through the use of the existing political process.

The early proponents of social democracy claimed that they were only revising Marxism. Their opponents, the defenders of Marxist orthodoxy, recognized that they were actually replacing Marxism with something entirely different. By the end of the nineteenth century socialism had split into two camps: the social democrats, who believed in the possibility of reform, and the communists, who still believed in revolution.

THE BEGINNINGS OF SOCIAL DEMOCRACY IN GERMANY

In the aftermath of the revolutions of 1848 Friedrich Wilhelm IV promulgated a constitution that included a legislature loosely based on the British parliament. Members of the upper house inherited their seats or were appointed by the king. Members of the lower house were elected by a variation on universal manhood suffrage. Voters were divided into three categories according to the amount of taxes they paid, with the votes of the wealthy more heavily weighted than the votes of the poor. The intention was to keep conservative landowners in power, but the plan backfired. By the end of the 1850s the vote was weighted in favor of wealthy manufacturers, merchants, bankers, and professionals.

With the rise to power of King Wilhelm I and his chancellor, Otto von Bismarck, Prussia, and by extension the lesser German states under its influence, entered a period of political change in the 1860s. Bismarck and the king, both moderate conservatives, found themselves in conflict with the newly powerful liberals. Since the working classes had at least a nominal vote, they often found themselves allied with the radical wing of the liberal movement.

Working-Class Organizations

The opportunities for working-class organizations were limited. Labor unions were illegal in all the German states, and there were heavy restrictions on the formation of political parties.

The primary model was the local workers' educational societies founded by liberals beginning in the 1840s as a way of supplementing low levels of primary education. In the 1860s workers began to take over these associations and run them on their own behalf. Most associations provided both lecture series and systematic courses designed to teach a specific subject. In 1864 alone the thirty-three education societies in Prussia sponsored more than one thousand public lectures. In 1866 many of these societies banded together to form the League of German Workingmen's Associations.

These groups provided the foundation for the first two social democratic workers' parties: the General German Workers' Association, established by Ferdinand Lassalle in 1863, and the German Social Democratic Party, founded by Wilhelm Liebknecht and August Bebel in 1869.

FERDINAND LASSALLE

Ferdinand Lassalle (1825–1864) was the son of a wealthy Jewish silk trader in Breslau. After eighteen unhappy months at a commercial school in Leipzig, he convinced his father to send him to the university instead. He spent two years at Breslau, studying philosophy, history, philology, and archaeology. He then transferred to Berlin, where he discovered Hegel and the French utopian socialists. Like Marx before him, he intended to pursue a career as a philosopher with the hope of transforming social conditions in Germany. Again like Marx, reality soon derailed his academic career.

Lassalle and the Countess

In 1846 Lassalle met Countess Sophie Hatzfeldt, who was trying to both divorce her husband and regain control of her fortune and her children. Over the course of eight years Lassalle filed thirty-five separate lawsuits in various courts on her behalf. After finally obtaining the divorce in 1854, the countess settled a pension on Lassalle, making him financially independent.

In March 1848, when revolution broke out in the German states, Lassalle was in jail in Düsseldorf as a result of his efforts in the Hatzfeldt case. Düsseldorf was an important center of the revolutionary struggle in the industrialized Rhineland. As soon as Lassalle was released from jail, he threw himself into the cause. He was not involved for long. The Düsseldorf authorities arrested him in November for an inflammatory speech urging the local military to revolt. He spent six months in jail.

Lassalle Founds a Political Party

Lassalle became a working-class leader almost by accident. From 1848 to 1857 Lassalle lived in Düsseldorf. During this period he corresponded regularly with Marx, continued his legal battle on behalf of the countess, and wrote on philosophical topics that hovered on the edge of socialism. He came to the conclusion that the battle for democracy had to be fought by the workers through working-class organizations.

In 1859 Lassalle left Düsseldorf for Berlin, where he worked as a political journalist and gave an occasional lecture at one of the educational societies. In 1862 he gave two addresses that fired the imagination of his listeners.

Lassalle soon got the chance to speak to a larger audience. Following a visit by German workers to the London International Exhibition of 1862, the educational societies of Berlin and Leipzig called a general congress of German workers. The program committee asked Lassalle to explain his views on the labor problem. They were especially interested in what he had to say about the ideas of Hermann Schulze-Delitzsch regarding cooperative credit unions.

The committee got more than they were expecting. Lassalle responded with an "Open Letter of Reply," in which he declared that universal suffrage was the only means to improve the material situation of the working class. He believed that cooperative credit associations or consumer cooperatives would accomplish little because David Ricardo's "iron law of wages" inevitably shaped the workers' place in a capitalist society.

Subsistence Level

According to Ricardo, the free market will always keep laborers' wages at a subsistence level. Wages will rise and fall in relationship to the cost of food, but capital will never pay more than a cost of living increase because a real wage increase comes directly out of profits.

Lassalle argued that workers would be better off establishing producers' cooperatives than consumer cooperatives. Instead of banding together to buy goods at a wholesale cost, workers should become their own employers through producers' cooperatives, thereby taking a first step toward abolishing the profit system, and ultimately ending the iron law of wages. If workers wanted to make a real change in society, they should create not only small workshops but also modern factories using capital advanced by the state. None of those changes could occur until workers lobbied for the first, most important, change. Before the state could become an instrument of reform, the working class must have the vote.

Lassalle's audience received the "Open Letter" as a call to action. Almost without effort on his part, the first working-class political organization, the General German Workers' Association, was founded in May 1863, with Lassalle as its president.

THE GERMAN SOCIAL DEMOCRATIC PARTY (SPD)

Several years after Lassalle's death, August Bebel (1840–1913) and Wilhelm Liebknecht (1826–1900) formed a second working-class political party in Germany, the German Social Democratic Party (SPD). Bebel was the son of a noncommissioned officer in the Prussian army. He was orphaned early in life and grew up in poverty. After traveling for several years as a journeyman woodworker, he settled in Leipzig, where he became involved in the local workers' educational society.

Liebknecht was an old-style radical who took refuge in London after the Revolutions of 1848. In London he joined the Communist League, where he worked closely with Marx and Engels and supported himself as a correspondent for the *Augsburg Gazette*. In 1862, when the Prussian government offered a general amnesty to those who had been involved in the Revolutions of 1848, he returned to Berlin. Fresh from the fount of Marxist wisdom in London,

Liebknecht quickly developed a following among the radical element of working-class Berlin. Just as quickly Bismarck had him thrown back out of Prussia. This time he went only as far as Leipzig, where he joined Lassalle's General German Workers' Association and met August Bebel.

In 1867 Liebknecht and Bebel were both elected to the constituent assembly for the newly formed North German Confederation. Although both were dedicated Marxists, they held their seats as part of the German People's Party, which was primarily made up of middle-class radicals.

The North German Confederation

The North German Confederation, a union of German states north of the Main River, was formed in 1867 with Berlin as its capital, King Wilhelm I as its president, and Bismarck as its chancellor. In 1871 the North German Confederation became the German Reich.

Bebel and Liebknecht soon came to the conclusion that they would command more respect on the legislative floor if they represented a Marxist organization comparable to the General German Workers' Association. They followed Lassalle's example and turned to the workers' education societies. Bebel had previously served as the chairman of the Leipzig Workers' Educational Association. In 1868 he was elected president of the Federation of Workingmen's Associations. Under his presidency the federation passed a resolution committing the federation to the program of the First International. The following year Bebel and Liebknecht issued an invitation to a German Social Democratic Workers' Congress in Eisenach, out of which the German Social Democratic Party was formed, with Bebel as its chairman.

GERMAN SOCIALISTS FACE BACKLASH

The violence of the Paris Commune of 1871 caused a backlash against socialism throughout Europe, especially in the new German Reich, where there were two well-established political parties professing socialistic and democratic principles. Fear of socialism on the part of the ruling classes was made worse in 1873, when Europe was hit with another severe economic depression, brought on in part by the financial consequences of the Franco-Prussian War. Once again businesses failed, domestic prices and wages fell, and unemployment rose. Fearful of a repetition of 1848, the police and the courts began to crack down on socialist organizations.

The Crash of 1873

The Long Depression began with the fall of the Viennese Stock Exchange on May 9, 1873. The crash set off a period of economic stagnation that continued for two decades. Despite slowed growth and rising unemployment, many members of the working classes actually enjoyed an increased standard of living during this period as a result of a steady fall in the cost of food and manufactured goods.

By 1875 the combination of increasing government persecution and the financial strain of unemployed members had made survival hard for both of Germany's socialist parties. Despite differences in organization and policy, the two organizations agreed to merge. Their leaders met in Gotha, where they created a charter for the new organization, known as the Gotha Program. The new organization, the German Social Democratic Party (SPD), was the largest of the pre-1914 Marxist parties. By 1912 the SPD was the largest single party represented in the Reichstag, the German parliament, holding 110 out of 397 seats.

Marx bitterly denounced the merger in his *Critique of the Gotha Program*, published posthumously by Engels in 1891. He complained that Lassalle had "conceived the workers' movement from the narrowest national standpoint," concentrating on converting Germany to socialism. Marx believed that socialism must be an international movement if it were to succeed. Worse, from Marx's perspective, Lassalle and his followers sought to gain control of the state through elections in the hope of transforming capitalism through the establishment of workers' collectives. Marx believed that the only path to socialism was through revolution.

Evolution or Revolution?

The question of whether the proletariat should bring about the socialist state through evolutionary reforms or violent revolution was one of the most debated in socialist circles until the Russian Revolution of 1917 caused the final split between the Social Democratic Party and the Communist Party.

BISMARCK'S ANTI-SOCIALIST LAWS

In 1878 Bismarck forced the passage of an anti-socialist law through the Reichstag. Socialist organizations, educational programs, and publications were banned, and arrest warrants were issued for individual socialist leaders.

Bebel told his fellow representatives in the Reichstag that passage of the bill would change nothing: "Your lances will be shattered in this struggle like glass on granite." In the long run he was right. When the law expired in 1890, the SPD won 20 percent of the popular vote, making Bebel the most prominent opponent of the government.

In the short run the SPD went underground, camouflaged by local clubs of various sorts. Contact between the clubs was maintained through a magazine, *The Social Democrat*. Published in Switzerland, thousands of copies were smuggled into Germany each week, each one forming the nucleus for a circle of readers that temporarily replaced the normal party organization.

THE ERFURT PROGRAM

In 1891 the SPD adopted a new charter, the Erfurt Program. The Gotha Program was a compromise between the overlapping ideologies of the two original parties. The Erfurt Program displayed signs of a more fundamental tension between revisionism and Marxist orthodoxy that had developed within the party.

Karl Kautsky, a defender of Marxist orthodoxy, drafted the first, theoretical, section of the program. In it, he stressed the division of society into two hostile camps and painted a grim picture of a future in which a few large-scale capitalist enterprises expand their control over the economic system.

Eduard Bernstein, a leading theoretician of social democratic revisionism, drafted the second, practical, portion of the program, which consisted of a series of reforms that could be obtained only by working within the system, including that perennial favorite, universal manhood suffrage, secularized schools, compensation for elected officials, and more liberal labor laws.

The official position was that the Erfurt Program was both reformist and revolutionary, combining immediate benefits for the proletariat with the long-term goal of overthrowing capitalism.

BERNSTEIN AND MARXIST REVISIONISM

A Heretic Lifts His Head

Social democracy found its theorist in Eduard Bernstein (1850–1932). Called "the father of revisionism," Bernstein built on Lassalle's ideas to produce what would become the basic ideology of social democracy.

"Revisionism" and Orthodoxy

After the Bolshevik Revolution communists began to use the term *revisionism* to attack what they saw as deviations from the Soviet norm. For instance, Josip Broz Tito's policies in communist Yugoslavia were condemned as "modern revisionism" by the Soviets. (Ironically, Communist China used the same term against Soviet Russia.)

Like Bebel, Bernstein was born into a working-class family and had personal experience of poverty. His father was a railroad engineer who did not make enough to support his ten surviving children. His uncle was the editor of the *Berlin People's Times*, a newspaper widely read in progressive working-class circles.

Bernstein attended the local school until he was sixteen, when he took an apprenticeship as a bank clerk. In 1872 he was introduced to socialist ideas by the highly publicized political trial of Bebel and Liebknecht, who were the only two members of the North German Reichstag who refused to vote for war bonds to fund the Franco-Prussian War. The leaders of the German Social Democratic Party used their defense as an opportunity to preach the socialist gospel and made at least one convert: Bernstein.

FROM SWITZERLAND TO LONDON

In 1878 Bernstein was one of the leaders indicted through Bismarck's anti-socialist laws. With a warrant issued for his arrest, he emigrated to Switzerland, where he became the editor of *The Social Democrat*. Expelled from Switzerland at Bismarck's insistence in 1888, he moved to London, where he became Friedrich Engels's right-hand man—chosen to produce the fourth volume of *Capital* from Marx's badly organized notes and designated the literary executor for Engels's estate.

While in London Bernstein also met the leaders of the newly formed Fabian Society, Sidney and Beatrice Webb. Under the Webbs' influence he came to realize that he no longer believed in many of Marx's arguments.

The Fabian Society

The London-based Fabian Society was founded in 1884 with the goal of establishing a democratic socialist state in Great Britain. The Fabians advocated a gradualist approach to social change, concentrating on education and participation in parliamentary politics. Members of the Fabian Society were instrumental in the formation of the British Labour Party.

EVOLUTIONARY SOCIALISM

In 1899, faced with a growing gap between the SPD's official ideology of Marxist class struggle and the reality of its parliamentary participation, Bernstein published socialism's most comprehensive theoretical critique of Marxist orthodoxy, *Evolutionary Socialism*. In it, Bernstein rejected two of the key elements of Marxist orthodoxy: historical materialism and class struggle. Instead of waiting for capitalism to collapse, he called on socialists to adapt the tools of parliamentary democracy and participation in government to achieve socialist ends. Instead of class struggle, he urged political cooperation between the working classes, the peasantry, and the dissatisfied members of the middle classes, all of whom suffered from the injustices of capitalism.

A Slow Progress

Bernstein is famous for the comment that "what is termed the final goal of socialism is nothing to me, the movement is everything." He meant that lasting social revolution comes through steady advances, "the ground gained piecemeal by hard, unremitting struggle, rather than through violent upheaval."

Bernstein ended with the conclusion that socialism was not the inevitable product of a revolt against capitalism. It was instead "something that ought to be." The success of socialism didn't depend on the continued and intensifying misery of the working classes but on eliminating that misery. The task for socialism was to develop suggestions for reform that would improve the living conditions of most people. And, as Lassalle had argued thirty-five years earlier, the first step was universal suffrage. With the vote, the working classes could create a socialist state by electing socialist representatives to a democratic government, making democracy both the means and the end.

SYNDICALISM AND TRADE UNIONS

Strike! Strike!

Social democrats weren't the only socialists to reject Marxist ortho-doxy. Standing at the intersection between trade unionism and anar-chism, syndicalists believed that Marxism simply replaced capital-ist factory owners with state bureaucrats. They also rejected social democracy's efforts at working within the system. Caught between state oppression and the futility of politics, syndicalists believed that society could be transformed only through direct action by the work-ing classes themselves, using trade unions and the general strike as their tools.

WHAT IS SYNDICALISM?

Syndicalism was a militant form of trade unionism that combined the ideas of Marx, Proudhon, and Bakunin with the technique of collective action by workers. Syndicalists advocated workers taking over the means of the production as a first step in abolishing the state. Both the state and the capitalist system would be replaced by a new social order, with the local trade union as its basic unit of organization. The method generally favored for accomplishing this transformation was the general strike.

Syndicalists rejected social democracy's policy of reform through parliamentary politics *and* Marxism's reliance on a centralized state after the revolution. Political parties were incapable of producing fundamental change. The state was by its nature a tool of capitalist oppression.

Instead of reform or state socialism, syndicalists looked to revolution by the direct action of the workers. If the unions were not strong enough to risk a strike, their members would attack employers through boycotts and sabotage. The climax of direct action would be the general strike.

After the revolution a federation of trade unions and labor exchanges would replace the state.

Trade Union or Revolutionary Movement?

The word *syndicalism* comes from the French term for labor union: *syndicate* (not to be confused with the English *syndicate*, which is something totally different). In France, where the movement was born, *syndicalism* means plain vanilla trade unionism. In France the union-based socialist movement is called *revolutionary syndicalism* or *anarcho-syndicalism*.

SYNDICALISM AND TRADE UNIONISM

Syndicalism was born in the French trade union movement at the end of the nineteenth century. Industrial trade unions developed alongside socialism. Unlike the earlier craft unions, which represented workers with a shared set of skills, industrial unions were organized to represent large numbers of workers within a specific industry or region—skilled and unskilled, employed or unemployed. Like socialist parties, such unions were motivated by a clear sense of class consciousness, in the Marxist sense, and the desire to improve the lives of workers.

Despite their similarities, trade unions and socialist parties differed in how they worked for change. The unions' goals were immediate and practical: higher wages, shorter hours, the eight-hour day, better working conditions. Trade unions relied on economic, rather than political, methods. Their primary tools were collective bargaining power, their ability to supply aid to their members, and, as a last recourse, the strike.

Class Consciousness

The syndicalist idea of the "conscious minority" was related to the socialist idea of "false consciousness." The conscious few must work on behalf of an unconscious majority who support a system that is against their interests. There is an inherent contradiction in syndicalist thought between the idea of the conscious minority and the central role of the general strike.

Syndicalist-run unions, like other trade unions, used the tactics of collective bargaining and limited strikes to win immediate benefits for their members. Unlike mainstream trade unions, the principal function of the syndicalist trade union was not winning economic gains for its members but undermining the political order by means of direct action led by a "conscious minority."

Syndicalism and Anarchism

French trade unions were breeding grounds for anarchism from the beginning. Proud of the French revolutionary tradition, workers were suspicious of both government and industry. Many rejected social democracy as corrupt, ineffective—and German. When trade unions were made legal in France in 1884, the bulk of the members were anarchists in the Proudhon tradition.

In its purest form, anarchism is opposed not only to the state but also to all types of hierarchy and authority. Anarchists prefer small groups, from revolutionary cells to producers' cooperatives, linked together in a decentralized federation.

The marriage between trade unions and anarchism was uncomfortable. The small groups that anarchists preferred made ineffective trade unions. Some anarchists even feared that the large industrial trade unions would create powerful interest groups in a new society.

Like anarchists, syndicalists rejected organized government and the coercion of the state. They believed power could and should be achieved by the workers themselves, rather than through political parties and the state. Unlike anarchists, syndicalists considered that the basic building block of the ideal society would be trade unions rather than small local communities.

THE FEDERATION OF LABOR EXCHANGES

Shortly after trade unions were legalized in France in 1884, the government of Léon Gambetta created an institution to help connect employers with laborers seeking work: the labor exchanges (*bourses du travail*). The first exchange opened in Paris in 1887 in a building donated by the local municipal council. Parisian workers demanded the right to run the exchanges themselves. By 1907 there were 150 labor exchanges in cities across France.

Most of the exchanges were founded with the help of local municipalities and began as places where workers could present themselves for hire. In the hands of the trade unions, the labor exchanges developed into much more, combining the function of workers' club, placement service, and mutual aid society. Unions used the exchanges to steer job seekers away from centers of labor disputes, preventing them from becoming strikebreakers. Exchanges served as local labor councils that included all the unions of different trades in a given city. Many exchanges became institutions for working-class education: setting up libraries, museums of labor history, technical colleges, and schools for the education of workers' children.

In 1892 French municipal labor exchanges came together to form the Federation of Labor Exchanges, effectively creating a collective bargaining unit for their organizations. Under the leadership of Fernand Pelloutier, the Federation became an incubator for syndicalism.

FERNAND PELLOUTIER AND THE FEDERATION OF LABOR EXCHANGES

Although syndicalism had no obvious founder, Fernand Pelloutier (1867–1901) was the first person to clearly articulate syndicalist ideals. Pelloutier was involved in the anarchist movement for several years before he became operating secretary of the Federation of Labor Exchanges in 1895. Under his leadership, the exchanges took on additional functions, such as providing information on how to find work, how to join unions and cooperatives, and how to go on strike; where possible, exchanges were encouraged to publish their own newspapers and provide information about labor markets to interested proletarian organizations. The membership rose to more than 250,000.

Like Proudhon before him, Pelloutier believed that workers could be emancipated only by their own direct action. He went further than Proudhon by insisting that when the proletariat tried to protect its interests within the framework of the state and socialist political parties, the natural tendency to reach compromises would undermine its moral fiber. Instead, the working class needed to work toward the revolution through its own institutions: the trade unions and labor exchanges.

A New Education System

Pelloutier hoped that workers who were educated in schools created by the labor exchanges would build a new system of values in which technical skill and discipline were valued over wealth, comfort, and leisure. Like Saint-Simon, he believed that the new leaders of the producing class would form a technical elite.

Pelloutier envisioned the labor exchanges as the beginning of a new proletarian civilization centered on trade unions. Once workers gained control of the methods of production, unions and labor exchanges would play different roles in society.

The local trade union would be the basic unit of society, with the job of producing goods and services. Individual unions would coordinate production within a specific sector of the economy, defined either by region or industry. Unions would be linked together in a loose federation of the type visualized earlier by Proudhon.

Unions would send representatives to the labor exchanges, which would be responsible for coordinating efforts between the different sectors of production. The labor exchanges would function as decentralized planning bodies. They would gather and disseminate information on production matters and consumer interests, giving the unions an overarching view of the production process.

After Pelloutier's death in 1901 the Federation of Labor Exchanges merged with the Federation of Trade Unions to create the General Confederation of Labor (CGT), which was dominated by syndicalism until 1921.

GENERAL STRIKES

The idea of the general strike was based on the belief that the industrial economy cannot survive even a short disruption of basic services. (Anyone who has been in a major city when the garbage collectors go on strike will understand the concept.)

British radical William Benbow first proposed the idea of a month-long general strike in 1831, euphemistically calling it a "Grand National Holiday." Bakunists also considered a "Sacred Month" of collective work stoppage.

In the 1890s French syndicalists expanded the idea of the general strike. Earlier socialists had envisioned the general strike as an act of noncooperation designed to win a concession from government or business. In syndicalist thought the general strike became a "revolution of folded arms": a tactic for overthrowing the government by bringing the economy to a halt.

Some syndicalists argued that every small strike was a skirmish in the larger class struggle. At least in theory this meant that it didn't matter whether a "partial" strike for higher wages or an eight-hour day succeeded or failed because the very act of striking was a blow against the capitalist system.

During the heyday of syndicalism, between 1900 and 1914, syndicalist groups attempted general strikes in Italy, Belgium, Holland, and Sweden, usually at the cost of violent response by the governments.

Syndicalism Put to the Test

In 1906 the CGT scheduled a nationwide strike for May 1. Many hoped that it would prove to be the general strike that would bring down the government.

The strike was triggered prematurely on March 10 by a coal mine disaster at Courrières. A gas explosion killed between 1,060 and 1,300 miners. Rescue operations were slow, made more difficult by an unseasonable snowstorm. (The last thirteen survivors were recovered twenty days after the explosion.) More than 15,000 people attended the first funerals, creating an explosion of another sort. By March 13, 61,000 miners were on strike.

Miners' Fund

Funds collected for the miners became part of an official fund set up by law within four days of the explosion. Together, the various efforts collected 750,000 francs. (The daily wage for a miner was less than 6 francs.) Mine owners donated more than half the amount raised.

The Courrières explosion was one of the first disasters reported in the French popular press. Reporters from across the country competed for news from the mine and published appeals for humanitarian aid for the victims and their families. Newspapers couldn't print photographs, but picture postcards of the disaster and the survivors spread across the country. With public sympathy engaged, the CGT called for the planned strike to begin on March

18; hundreds of thousands of strikers joined the miners' demonstrations in Pas-de-Calais and Nord.

The minister of the interior, Georges Clemenceau, reacted quickly to suppress the strikes, flooding the region with troops and arresting seven hundred union leaders.

The Charter of Amiens

The ferocity of the government's response left many union members shaken. When the CGT Congress met at Amiens later that year, several argued that the unions should abandon the idea of direct action, follow the lead of the democratic socialists, and lobby for change through the political system. The proposal was rejected. Representatives at the Congress passed a resounding vote of support for syndicalist ideas. The broad resolution, known as the Charter of Amiens, is perhaps the clearest and most influential statement of syndicalist ideals:

> In the daily fight, Syndicalism pursues the co-ordination of workers' struggles, and the increase of working class welfare through the achievement of immediate reforms such as a decrease in the hours of the working day, increased salaries, etc....But this task is only one aspect of Syndicalism, which also prepares the ground for complete emancipation. This can only be realized by the expropriation of the capitalists through the General Strike. The trade union, which today is a defensive institution, will be, in the future, the basis of production, distribution and the reorganisation of society.

SOCIALISTS IN WORLD WAR I

The End of the Second International

In the summer of 1914 socialism seemed to have reached the acme of power. Socialists were members of parliament in France and Germany, holding significant blocs of votes. The socialist movement in Great Britain was growing in strength; even in the United States organizations such as the Industrial Workers of the World, a syndicalist organization strongly influenced by socialist ideology, had enrolled thousands of workers in their ranks.

Many commentators remarked that that summer was the most perfect in memory.

But in June a Serbian nationalist assassinated Archduke Franz Ferdinand and his wife while they were visiting the Serbian town of Sarajevo. Franz Ferdinand was the heir to the Austro-Hungarian empire, and the empire's rulers demanded that Serbia be annexed to the empire. Serbia appealed for support to Russia, with which it had a treaty of protection. Germany announced its support of Austro-Hungary, while Britain and France sided with Russia. By August 1914 guns were sounding all over Europe. The First World War had begun.

THE GERMAN CRISIS

In the run-up to the war the deputies to the Reichstag who were members of the Social Democratic Party announced that they would not support war credits and would vote against any move by the government to go to war. However, with the outbreak of war they reversed their position and voted in favor of the government's request for war credits.

Karl Liebknecht

Among the socialist members of the Reichstag was Karl Liebknecht (1871–1919), son of Wilhelm Liebknecht, cofounder of the German Social Democratic Party (SPD). Karl was the only member of the Reichstag to vote against war credits (110 members of the SPD at that time occupied positions in the Reichstag). After the war Liebknecht formed the Spartacus League with several other left-leaning socialists, including Rosa Luxemburg (1871–1919). In the chaos following the end of the war, they attempted to launch an uprising against the new German government. The uprising was suppressed with the aid of right-leaning militias called *Freikorps*. Liebknecht and Luxemburg were arrested by members of the *Freikorps* and swiftly murdered.

The nationalist turn of the German SPD was mirrored by the French adherents of the International. For all intents and purposes, the Second International was now dead, since its members were literally shooting at one another from the trenches that crisscrossed France. There was an attempt to revive its spirit at a conference in Zimmerwald in neutral Switzerland in 1915, but it failed to accomplish much.

THE ZIMMERWALD MOVEMENT

The Zimmerwald Conference of 1915 was only the first of several efforts to unite those members of the various socialist parties in

Europe who still believed in internationalism and opposed participation in World War I. Although unsuccessful, it did clearly demonstrate the differences between revolutionary and gradualist tendencies in the International.

Among those attending the first conference was Grigory Zinoviev on behalf of the Bolshevik faction of the Russian Social-Democratic Workers' Party. Representatives were also present from the Mensheviks, the Italian Socialist Party, and the Polish socialists. Lenin did not take part in the proceedings, although he drafted several resolutions for consideration by the conference. Trotsky took part in the conference in a position halfway between the Bolsheviks and Mensheviks.

Trotsky—Half and Halfway

To Lenin's extreme annoyance, Trotsky continued to try to balance between the Bolshevik and Menshevik factions. Although he often leaned left, as he did at Zimmerwald, he never fully committed to Lenin's side. This maneuvering continued right up until early 1917, when Trotsky, having returned to Russia, finally joined the Bolsheviks.

The Conference quickly divided between those who wanted to denounce the war, those who had voted for it and supported it, and those who wanted to take a more moderate stance. In the end the Conference formed an International Socialist Commission, which functioned as a kind of clearinghouse for those members of the Second International who did not support the war. The final resolution passed was so watered-down as to be meaningless.

Lenin's View

Lenin regarded the Zimmerwald Movement as evidence that the old social democratic structure was dead and needed to be replaced. A new international organization was needed, in his opinion, and he and Zinoviev would act on this in 1919 by founding the Third (Communist) International.

Many Internationals

As discussed later, the Third International lasted until the Second World War, when it was reorganized as the Communist Information Bureau (Cominform). Followers of Trotsky organized a Fourth International in 1938, but it remained relatively small, and split on several occasions.

THE BEGINNING OF THE RUSSIAN REVOLUTION

1905 and February 1917

Marx predicted that the end of capitalism would begin in mature industrial societies. The merciless dialectic between capital and labor would bring the internal conflicts of capitalism to the breaking point, and outraged labor would revolt against their misery. Instead, the first avowedly Marxist revolution took place in Tsarist Russia, where the proletariat formed only a small portion of the population, but there was plenty of misery to go around.

WHAT WAS IT LIKE IN RUSSIA IN 1900?

In 1900 Russia looked disturbingly like France in 1789. Tsar Nicholas II (1894–1917) and the Orthodox Church still believed in the divine right of kings. Nicholas was the last of Europe's absolute monarchs: unfettered by constitutional restraints or parliamentary institutions. The population was largely divided between wealthy aristocrats and struggling peasants, with only a small middle class in the cities. The gulf between rich and poor was enormous. But things were starting to change.

Russia Begins an Industrial Revolution

Russia took its first steps toward industrialization in 1856, after the Crimean War made it clear that modern wars were won with railroads and industrial capacity. The process was slow at first, but by the 1880s Russia was finally in the grip of the Industrial Revolution, with a few peculiarly Russian twists.

In Western Europe the Industrial Revolution began with small workshops. Enterprises grew larger over time as a new industrial class emerged and accumulated both the capital and the knowledge for economic development.

By the time Russia entered the game, the time of small workshops was long over. Without a homegrown base of capital and expertise, the Industrial Revolution started from the top down. The tsarist government was a large entrepreneur in its own right, responsible for constructing a railroad network across the country and a major player in the development of the coal and iron industries. For the most part the landowning aristocracy had no interest in investing in industry, so much of the capital came from abroad. By 1900 more than 50 percent of the capital in Russian manufacturing companies was foreign. In crucial industries, like iron, the percentage was even higher.

Peasants and the Proletariat

Russia could only dream of having an urban proletariat in 1900. The tsar's grandfather, Alexander II (1818–1881), emancipated the serfs in 1861, in part to make it possible for peasants to emigrate to the cities and become industrial workers. Emancipation tied former serfs to the land in new ways. The process by which land was distributed to the peasants required them to "redeem" the land from its former owners over a forty-nine-year period. Ownership was further complicated by the traditional village commune, known as the *mir*. The self-governing units held the land in common, and allotments were redistributed periodically to ensure economic equality. Before emancipation the *mir* was responsible for taxes and obligations to the landlord; after emancipation the *mir* was responsible for taxes and redemption payments to the landlord. A peasant who wanted to move to the city had to give up all claim to the land or return to work the harvest.

The End of Serfdom

Prior to the Emancipation Manifesto of 1861 Russian peasants were legally tied to the land they were born on: not quite slaves but certainly not free. The Manifesto gave roughly 23 million people the rights of full citizens, including the right to marry without their landlord's consent, to leave the land, and to own property or a business.

The Russian proletariat had plenty to complain about. The fact that they had to return to the country for the harvest meant that many of them were transient workers who took whatever unskilled jobs were available. Wages were extremely low, even by the standards of other proletariats: in 1880 a factory worker in Moscow earned only a quarter of the wage earned by his British counterpart. With no tradition of personal freedom, many workers were treated like industrial serfs, housed in barracks and marched back and forth to work each day.

Political parties and trade unions were illegal. Even professional associations were highly regulated and their meetings were supervised. One of the few legal forms of organization was the *zemstvo*, a type of elected regional council established by Alexander II. Controlled by the nobility, *zemstvos* were legally limited to dealing with local and charitable issues, though some liberal-minded aristocrats attempted to extend the councils' scope to include political matters.

Newspapers, magazines, and books, both those published in Russian and those imported from abroad, were rigorously censored.

Political literature had to be secretly printed and distributed. It was often published by political émigrés and smuggled into the country.

All opposition parties—reformers and revolutionaries alike—worked underground, shadowed by the threat of imprisonment, exile to Siberia, or execution. With no other outlet for voicing opposition, assassination attempts against members of the royal family and high government officials were common. Secret police infiltrated opposition groups, and revolutionaries offered themselves as police spies to find out about police plans.

THE FIRST RUSSIAN REVOLUTION

At the end of 1904 Russia was buckling under the Japanese. At first glance the Russo-Japanese conflict looked like a David and Goliath fight, but in fact the least industrialized of the European powers didn't have a chance against the newly industrialized Japanese.

The Russo-Japanese War

The Russo-Japanese War began with Japan's attack on the Russian naval base at Port Arthur in Manchuria on February 9, 1904, and ended with the destruction of the Russian fleet in the Tsushima Straits on May 27, 1905. Officially, the war was a conflict over who controlled Manchuria and Korea. Unofficially, it was Japan's debut as an international power.

In addition to the sting of national humiliation, the war placed an immense strain on Russia's fragile infrastructure. While the government concentrated on the difficult task of supplying its armed forces in Asia, the systems for provisioning Russia's large cities broke down. The price of essential goods rose so quickly that real wages fell by 20 percent.

Worker Protests

Worker discontent boiled over in December 1904, when the Putilov Iron Works in St. Petersburg began to lay off workers. The Putilov workers went on strike, soon joined by thousands of workers in other parts of the city. The government responded by cutting off electricity to the city, shutting down newspapers, and declaring public areas of the city closed.

"Bloody Sunday"

On January 22 more than 150,000 Russian workers, many of them women and children, marched peacefully on the Winter Palace in St. Petersburg. Calling on their "Little Father" for help in difficult times, the workers tried to present Tsar Nicholas II with a petition demanding the usual political and economic reforms, including a popularly elected assembly, improved working conditions, better wages, reduced hours, universal manhood suffrage—and the end of the war with Japan. The Imperial Guard blocked the way and fired on the crowd to keep them from moving forward. Between bullets and the panicking crowd, more than one hundred people were killed or wounded.

News of what was predictably called "Bloody Sunday" set off insurrections and activism at every level of society. Middle-class professional associations and aristocratically controlled *zemstvos* called for a constituent assembly. Students walked out of universities in protest against the lack of civil liberties. Village *mirs* organized uprisings against landholders. Industrial workers went on strike.

More Insurrection

In June, soon after the Japanese destruction of the Russian fleet, the spirit of insurrection infected the military. Sailors on the battleship *Potemkin* protested against being served rotten meat. When the captain ordered the ringleaders shot, the firing squad refused to carry out his orders and the crew threw their officers overboard. Other units of the army and navy followed the *Potemkin*'s example.

In October the railway workers went on strike, paralyzing transportation. At the same time the Mensheviks and other parties set up a workers' council (known as a Soviet) in St. Petersburg to coordinate revolutionary activities. Within a matter of weeks more than fifty Soviets had been formed in towns and cities across Russia. Leon Trotsky eventually became head of the Petrograd soviet.

Soviet

The term *soviet* originally referred to a council of any kind. The workers' Soviets created in the 1905 revolution were made up of elected representatives from each factory or workshop in a town. Soviets became the basic units of government at the local and regional level in the Union of Soviet Socialist Republics.

The Tsar's Response

Faced with general unrest, the tsar's chief minister recommended that Nicholas create an elected legislative assembly as a way to appease the public. The tsar reluctantly agreed. He issued the October Manifesto on October 17, which established a limited form of constitutional monarchy in Russia and guaranteed fundamental civil liberties. The most important provision of the manifesto was the implementation of a new advisory council, the *Duma*, which would be chosen by popular election and would have the authority to approve or reject all legislation.

Radicals found the fact that the *Duma* would be only a consulting body, not a true legislature, hard to swallow. The leaders of the St. Petersburg Soviet denounced the plan and were arrested.

Backlash

The October Manifesto resulted in a conservative backlash. Between 1906 and 1914 armed bands known as the Black Hundreds organized pogroms, took punitive action against peasants who were involved in the insurrections, and attacked students and activists. The Black Hundreds were drawn from those invested in the old system: landowners, rich peasants, bureaucrats, merchants, police officers, and Orthodox clergy.

Radical doubts about the proposed *Duma* were well founded. When the Fundamental Laws that detailed the structure of the new reforms were released in April 1906, the shape of the *Duma* was radically altered. The right to vote was severely limited. The elected *Duma* was now the lower house of a two-house chamber with only limited control over legislature. Members of the upper house were appointed by the tsar, who retained the right to rule by decree when the *Duma* wasn't in session.

Between 1906 and 1917 four separate *Dumas* were convened. Liberal and socialist groups dominated the first two *Dumas*, which proposed a series of reforms, including universal manhood suffrage, lifting the restrictions on trade unions, and land reform. Each time, the *Duma* remained in session for only a few months before Nicholas shut them down.

The First World War destroyed whatever faith the Russian people still had in the tsarist government. Ill-equipped and badly led, Russia suffered defeat after defeat, mostly at the hands of Germany. By the end of 1915 one million Russian soldiers had been killed, and another one million had been captured.

The government was equally inept at organizing the home front. Its greatest failure was an inability to organize food distribution, creating rising prices and artificial food shortages in the cities.

THE FEBRUARY 1917 REVOLUTION

On February 2, 1917, Petrograd, as St. Petersburg was then called, was in the throes of a general strike. The transportation system had failed, so there was no way to distribute the food that sat in the city's warehouses. The streets were crowded with people standing in food lines in the bitter cold.

When the inevitable bread riot broke out, the police fired on the crowd. Everything was business as usual until the army unit that was sent to reinforce the police instead disarmed them and joined the strikers. Suddenly the bread riot was a full-scale rebellion.

Is It Petersburg, Petrograd, or Leningrad?

It depends on when you're talking about. Peter the Great founded the city in 1703, claiming that he named it after his patron saint. In 1914 the name became Petrograd because many Russians thought St. Petersburg sounded too German. In 1924 the city became Leningrad in Lenin's honor. In 1991 residents voted to change the name back to St. Petersburg.

It took several days for the news to reach Tsar Nicholas, who insisted on staying with the army at the front. It apparently took a little longer to make him understand that this was more than just another bread riot. Finally, under pressure from both the *Duma* and his senior military officers, Tsar Nicholas abdicated in favor of his brother, the Grand Duke Michael Alexandrovich. The Grand Duke, apparently quicker on the uptake than his brother, declined to accept the throne.

The *Duma* quickly established a provisional government made up of the leaders of all the bourgeois parties. At the same time the leaders of the Russian Social-Democratic Workers' Party organized the Petrograd Soviet of Workers' and Soldiers' Deputies: 2,500 elected representatives from factories and military units around the city.

LENIN AND THE RUSSIAN REVOLUTION

The Bolsheviks Act

The Russian Social-Democratic Workers' Party was founded in 1898, with the intention of bringing together Russian Marxists in a single organization. Unity didn't last long. At the organization's second congress, held in Brussels and London in 1903, party members found themselves divided over two related questions:

- Should party membership be limited to active revolutionaries?
- Could a socialist revolution occur in a country that was still in the initial stages of capitalism?

The debate split the party into two factions: the Bolshevik (majority) party, led by Vladimir Lenin, and the Menshevik (minority) party, led by George Plekhanov and Pavel Axelrod.

The Minority As Majority

It is typical of the complicated relationship between the two groups that the Menshevik faction actually represented the majority of the Social-Democratic Workers' Party. The names came about as a result of a questionable vote at the 1903 congress that gave Lenin's faction control of the party for a short time. The Mensheviks quickly regained control, but the names stuck.

Although both groups claimed to be Marxist, there were fundamental differences in their approaches to revolution. The Mensheviks took an approach halfway between revisionist and orthodox Marxism. They believed that Russia could achieve socialism only after it developed into a bourgeois society with an oppressed proletariat. Until the budding Russian proletariat was fully developed and ready for revolution, they were willing to cooperate with nonsocialist liberals to implement reforms. The Bolsheviks were prepared to adapt Marxism to fit Russian political realities. Unlike the Mensheviks, they recognized that the peasants were as oppressed as any urban proletariat and represented a potential revolutionary force.

THE SOCIALIST REVOLUTIONARY PARTY

The Russian Social-Democratic Workers' Party wasn't the only game in town for would-be Russian revolutionaries. The Socialist Revolutionary Party, founded in 1901, worked chiefly among the rural population. The Marxist-based Social-Democrats looked forward to a socialist state based on the industrialized working class. The Socialist Revolutionaries hoped that Russia could bypass capitalism, or at least limit its scope. They proposed building a socialist country based on the traditional village *mir*. The land would be nationalized, but it would be worked by peasants on the principle of "labor ownership": a cross between squatters' rights and sweat equity.

VLADIMIR LENIN: ARCHITECT OF THE BOLSHEVIK REVOLUTION

Vladimir Lenin (1870–1924) was born into a middle-class family of educators in a small city near Moscow. When Lenin was a young teenager, his older brother was executed for conspiring to assassinate Tsar Alexander III. After the death of his brother, Lenin began to study revolutionary ideas. By the time he was seventeen he was already in trouble with the Russian authorities for participating in an illegal student rally. He was expelled from the university system and banished to his grandfather's estate, where his older sister was already under house arrest.

Pseudonyms

Lenin's original name was Vladimir Ulyanov. After his return from Siberia he used a number of aliases as part of his clandestine political work. In 1902 he adopted the pseudonym "Lenin," which was derived from the Lena River in Siberia.

In 1893, after taking his law exams and being admitted to the bar, Lenin moved to St. Petersburg, where he worked as a public defender. He became involved in unifying the city's various Marxist groups into a single organization known as the Union for the Struggle for the Liberation of the Working Class. The Union issued leaflets pleading the workers' cause, supported strikes, and collaborated with workers' educational societies.

That sort of thing never went over well with absolutist rulers. In December 1895 the Union's leaders were arrested. Lenin spent fifteen months in jail in St. Petersburg, and then was exiled to Siberia for three years.

At the end of his term in Siberia Lenin joined the Russian expatriate community, living at various times in Munich, London, and Geneva. During this period he cofounded the newspaper *Iskra* (*The Spark*) and published books and pamphlets about revolutionary politics.

What Is to Be Done?

Much of the debate at the 1903 congress of the Russian Social-Democratic Workers' Party was based on one of Lenin's most important books: *What Is to Be Done?* (1902). In it, Lenin proposed that the party should be the "vanguard of the proletariat," serving the same purpose in class warfare as the vanguard does in a military war.

Bolshevism and Syndicalism

Lenin's idea of the "vanguard of the proletariat" is similar to the syndicalist idea of the "conscious minority." Both ideas assume that a more enlightened group must lead the proletariat to revolution. Lenin's "vanguard of the proletariat" would include members of the "bourgeois intelligentsia." The syndicalist "conscious minority" would be members of the labor elite.

Marx and Engels claimed that the working class would emancipate itself; Lenin argued that the working class, left to itself, would develop "trade union consciousness," not "revolutionary consciousness." It was necessary for a vanguard of what Lenin called the "bourgeois intelligentsia" to lead the proletariat in the revolution, and for a hierarchical, strictly disciplined communist party to lead the intelligentsia. No one doubted that Lenin, himself, would lead the party.

LENIN AND THE BOLSHEVIK TAKEOVER

Lenin returned from exile on April 3, 1917, a month after the tsar abdicated, and immediately became a leading voice in the Bolshevik Party. (Bolsheviks and Mensheviks had, by this time, more or less formally split into two parties.) Most Bolsheviks still believed that it was impossible for a socialist revolution to take place in a country that was in the first stages of the Industrial Revolution. Lenin took the position that the revolution did not solve the fundamental problems of the Russian proletariat, and the task ahead was to turn the bourgeois revolution into a proletarian one.

In May Lenin gained an ally when Leon Trotsky, a leading figure of Russian socialism, returned from exile in the United States and joined the Bolshevik Party. By June Lenin and Trotsky had formed an alliance and begun to plot the overthrow of the provisional government.

On October 24, 1917, the Bolsheviks staged a relatively bloodless coup, with soldiers from the Soviet taking control of strategic points throughout Petrograd. The following day the all-Russian Congress of Soviets approved the formation of a revolutionary Bolshevik government with Lenin at its head.

Sir Thomas More (1478–1535) published one of the earliest visions of a new society, one that inspired many future socialist thinkers. His book *Utopia* envisioned a society in which everyone worked on equal terms in a series of agrarian communities. All property was shared in common, and no type of work was held to be better than another.

The Industrial Revolution of the late eighteenth and early nineteenth centuries expanded the production of goods. However, it also concentrated the industrial working class in unhealthy urban slums, where they suffered from disease and malnutrition. It was not until late in the nineteenth century that the urban poor, often led by socialist agitators, began to win significant concessions from capitalist entrepreneurs.

German philosopher Karl Marx (1818–1883), together with his colleague and friend Friedrich Engels (1820–1895), created modern scientific socialism (called "scientific" to distinguish it from the previous "utopian" socialism of other writers—Marx argued that his socialism was based on the inevitable movement of economic forces, not moral objections to capitalism). In 1848 Marx and Engels wrote *The Communist Manifesto*, a blast of their ideas intended to mobilize the industrial working class of Europe. Marx spent much of the rest of his life in London, where he wrote his masterpiece, *Capital*.

Photo Credit: © Wikimedia Commons

This page: In 1871, in the wake of France's defeat in the Franco-Prussian War, soldiers and workers erected barricades in the streets of Paris and fought pitched battles against the National Guard for control of the city. For a brief time they formed a socialist commune in which the people ruled and the wealthy lost their privileges. Although they were eventually defeated with much bloodshed, the Paris Commune was regarded by socialists as a significant example of the power of a revolutionary uprising.

Opposite page, bottom: Worker and peasant uprisings swept Europe in 1848. The idealism of the young revolutionaries can be seen in Eugène Delacroix's masterpiece, *Liberty Leading the People*. Although they were defeated, they showed the growing power of the urban working class, which inspired socialist thinkers like Marx and Engels.

Crafty and secretive, Joseph Stalin (1878–1953) took power in the Soviet Union after defeating his chief rival, Leon Trotsky (1879–1940). While in power, Stalin enforced collectivization of agriculture, causing a massive famine, and constructed a totalitarian state. However, he also led the Soviet people to victory in World War II.

Photo Credit: © 123RF/Sergei Gorin

This page: Mao Zedong (1893–1976), depicted here leading workers and peasants, became the leader and dictator of China after defeating Chiang Kai-shek (1887–1975) in a civil war lasting from 1945 to 1949. He imposed various socialist measures, many of which improved the lives of China's working class. However, some were disastrous, such as the Great Leap Forward, an attempt to force rural China to create its own industrial base. The program set back agricultural progress for many years and brought no discernable benefits to the peasantry.

Opposite page, bottom: Vladimir Lenin (1870–1924) led the October 1917 Bolshevik Revolution in Russia. The revolution unseated the Russian Provisional Government, which had taken the reins of power after the collapse of the Tsarist regime in February 1917 but had been unable to fulfill the people's demands for peace, land, and bread. Lenin and the Bolsheviks were prepared to address these issues.

This page: In the period leading up to World War II, socialist organizations suffered a series of defeats, the most tragic of which was in Germany. The rise of fascism, an extreme and oppressive form of nationalism, meant that socialist groups such as the German Communist Party and the Social Democratic Party came under attack, and most of their members were imprisoned in concentration camps.

Opposite page, top: Today in many countries, particularly in Scandinavia, socialist forms of healthcare, from dentistry to eyecare to general care, are widespread. In such countries the costs of healthcare are covered by taxation; visits to the doctor do not require co-pays or fees.

American Eugene V. Debs (1855–1926) became a socialist in the 1890s while imprisoned for union activity. He was a passionate speaker, and as a socialist he sharply opposed US involvement in World War I. As a result of a June 1918 speech in Canton, Ohio (seen here), he was arrested and charged with advocating the overthrow of the government.

Although support for socialist ideas waned sharply during the 1950s as a result of the US witch hunt for "subversives" led by Senator Joseph McCarthy, it saw a revival in the 1960s. This was partly due to the civil rights movement and growing opposition among young people to the American government's role in the Vietnam War (seen here). As a result, in organizations such as Students for a Democratic Society, support for socialism in many different forms became widespread.

Photo Credit: © Wikimedia Commons

In recent years there has been a resurgence of socialism in the United States. Bernie Sanders, an openly democratic socialist candidate, vied for the 2016 and 2018 Democratic presidential nominations. Socialists have been elected to city councils around the country and to Congress. And the Democratic Socialists of America, active within the Democratic Party, has an announced membership of more than 50,000.

Photo Credit: © Wikimedia Commons

SOCIALISM IN POWER

Innovation and Struggles

The new Bolshevik regime started out well. On October 26 the temporary ruling council passed a series of decrees that addressed popular concerns with land distribution, economic equality, and the shape of the new government. The great estates would be partitioned and distributed to the peasant communes with compensation to the former owners. Workers were given control over factories. Banks were nationalized. Plans were put forward to elect a constituent assembly to replace the temporary council. The long-awaited socialist revolution was on its way.

On October 27 the revolution took a detour when the ruling council passed the Decree on the Press, censoring all Russian publications. In the coming weeks the temporary council passed further restrictive measures.

In December the *Cheka* (secret police) was established to discover and suppress any attempts at counterrevolution. When election results for the proposed constituent assembly were tallied in January 1918, the Bolsheviks found that they had won only 21 percent of the vote. Lenin followed the precedent set by Nicholas II and dissolved the assembly, saying that the choices were Bolshevik rule or the return of the extreme right.

Each new extension of power was justified as a temporary measure. After all, Russia was at war. Lenin understood that if his party were to have any hope of holding on to power, they would have to withdraw from the war.

Trotsky, appointed minister of foreign affairs, attempted to negotiate a favorable treaty with Germany. At last, under heavy pressure from Germany on one side and Lenin on the other, he signed the Treaty of Brest-Litovsk on March 3, 1918. The treaty made vast concessions to Germany:

- Russia withdrew its claims to the Baltic states of Finland, Estonia, Latvia, and Lithuania.
- Much of western Russia was occupied by German and Austro-Hungarian troops.
- Areas of the Caucasus to the south were also ceded to Germany.

Lenin was willing to give in on these points, partly because he saw it as essential to have peace at any price and partly because both he and Trotsky believed that in the aftermath of the war a socialist revolution would break out in Germany, making any territorial concessions meaningless.

The Workers' Flag Is Deepest Red

The identification of socialists as "reds" began with the flag of the Paris Commune of 1871. The Commune chose red in memory of the blood that was shed by French workers during one hundred years of revolution. It was also a symbol of equality, based on the idea that all men's blood is red.

As soon as Lenin signed a treaty with Germany, however, the newly formed Soviet Union found itself fighting a civil war against the counterrevolutionary Whites, made up of nationalists, aristocrats, and remnants of the tsarist army, financed by Russia's former allies.

Leon Trotsky was charged by the Soviet government with forming an army to counter the Whites' attacks. Using a combination of tsarist troops and commanders and volunteer workers and peasants, he forged the Red Army. Trotsky traveled with the army in a specially constructed armored train. Under his leadership, the Whites were defeated by 1921, though at tremendous cost to the new state. Starvation was widespread, and atrocities were committed by both sides during the war.

Foreign Troops in the Soviet Union

In addition to the White armies, foreign troops took part in the fighting during the civil war, although on a very limited scale. Forces from France, Italy, Great Britain, and the United States fought the communists before withdrawing by 1921.

When a member of the Socialist Revolutionary Party nearly succeeded in an attempt to assassinate Lenin in August 1918, the war against counterrevolutionaries was unleashed on the population as a whole in the form of the Red Terror. On Lenin's orders, the *Cheka* executed thousands of "opponents of the state" without trial.

WAR COMMUNISM

During the civil war, with the support of both Lenin and Trotsky, the Soviet Union experimented with a system called War Communism. The intention was to make sure that the cities, where the Bolsheviks believed their political strength lay, were supplied with food, even if this meant forcibly taking food from peasant families. As well, the government attempted to quickly implement a series of socialist policies:

- All industries were nationalized.
- Strikes were outlawed as being harmful during a time a war.

- There was rationing of food.
- Workers and peasants were required to work. "He who does not work shall not eat," Lenin wrote, adapting a verse from the Bible.

Following the war, the Bolsheviks admitted that the system had been largely a disaster. It spiked the resentment of the peasantry and made the gap between urban and rural areas wider. It also led to a severe drop in productivity (aided by the disruption of the civil war), and this was accompanied by malnutrition in many parts of the country.

Normal or Emergency

While Lenin saw War Communism as a temporary measure, designed to help the war effort, others, including Trotsky and party leader Nikolai Bukharin (1888–1938), believed that the country could transition through War Communism to the basic forms of socialist production, and that it could do so quickly.

THE NEW ECONOMIC POLICY

In 1921, recognizing that the situation was dire, Lenin proposed what became known as the New Economic Policy (NEP). Under the NEP, small businesses would be allowed but on a limited and strictly state-regulated basis. The Soviet government hoped to attract a measure of foreign investment through this policy, though this had limited success.

In the field of agriculture attempts at collectivization of peasant holdings were discontinued, and private ownership of land was allowed. The Soviet government was, however, extremely cautious about this. Peasants who acquired substantial tracts of land were called kulaks, and they were watched carefully to make sure they did not become a social force capable of challenging the state.

Kulaks

The term *kulak* dates back to the Russian empire; however, exactly what defined a kulak varied over time. Under the Bolsheviks, kulaks were deemed "class enemies" even as they were tolerated during the NEP. When Joseph Stalin began his campaign of peasant collectivization in the 1930s, *kulak* took on a more sinister meaning, and many thousands were sent to labor camps or killed outright.

During the struggle between Stalin and Trotsky, which took up much of party life in the late 1920s, Trotsky and the faction within the Bolshevik Party known as the Left Opposition expressed hostility toward the NEP, which they felt had the power to create a small capitalist center of opposition to Soviet rule. Stalin was generally supportive of the NEP (along with the much more enthusiastic Bukharin) but abruptly turned against it in the late 1920s after Trotsky had been defeated and sent into exile. In 1928 he launched the first Five-Year Plan, signaling the onset of a strictly centralized economy, and the NEP ceased to exist.

THE THIRD INTERNATIONAL

Formation of the Comintern

The Russian Revolution tore the socialist community in two. Many European socialists doubted whether the Bolshevik Revolution was really socialist. Lenin declared that democratic socialists were traitors and renegades. In January 1918 the Bolshevik party formally acknowledged the break between social democrats and communists by changing its name from the Russian Social-Democratic Workers' Party to the Russian Communist Party.

Zinoviev, Leader of the International

Although Lenin, Trotsky, and other Bolshevik leaders played a significant role in the founding of the Comintern, responsibility for running the organization largely fell to Grigory Zinoviev (1883–1936). Zinoviev had been one of the central leaders of the party, though he had strongly opposed the October 1917 Bolshevik Revolution. In the forthcoming conflict between Trotsky and Stalin he initially sided with Stalin and was forced out of the party in disgrace after Stalin triumphed. He was put on trial in 1936, found guilty of treason, and shot.

In 1919 Lenin preempted efforts by moderate socialist leaders to revive the Second International by creating his own international organization. In May 1919 Russia hosted the first meeting of the Communist International, also known as the Comintern, in Moscow. Unlike the First and Second Internationals, the Comintern accepted no variations in socialist philosophy. The organization's stated purpose was to promote the spread of the socialist revolution across the industrialized world. In order to be admitted to the Comintern, socialist parties were required to model themselves on the Bolshevik party pattern and expel moderate socialists and pacifists from their membership rolls.

Some thirty-seven organizations were invited to the founding conference. In some cases these included more than one organization from the same country. For example, from the United States delegates represented the Socialist Labor Party, left-leaning members of the Socialist Party (these would shortly break from the SP to form the Communist Party of the United States), the Industrial Workers of the World, and the Workers' International Industrial Union.

Bolshevik Leadership

As a successful revolutionary party possessing immense moral authority over the International, the Bolsheviks used their own experience in Russia to guide the delegates. In the underdeveloped world, for instance, they stressed the importance of forming an alliance with the peasantry, as they had tried to do in Russia.

Comintern agents were sent to various countries to foment revolution, generally without much success.

Béla Kun

Among the most widely known of the Comintern's agents was the Hungarian revolutionary Béla Kun (1886–1938). Kun was a prominent figure in the Hungarian Soviet Republic, formed in 1919. However, the Republic never controlled more than a third of Hungary's territory, and it collapsed after less than five months. Kun later took part in the governing of Crimea. During Stalin's purge trials in the 1930s he was tried for treason and shot.

After the battle between Stalin and Trotsky had been resolved in the former's favor, the Comintern became largely a means for the Soviet Union to impose its line on foreign communist parties. This led to disaster in Germany in the early 1930s, when Stalin was convinced that the social democrats represented a far greater threat than the Nazis (the German Communist Party referred scornfully to the social democrats as "social fascists").

During World War II the Comintern, having initially called for communists to take no position in the conflict between the Western allies and Hitler, switched its position literally overnight when the Germans invaded the Soviet Union in June 1941. As a gesture of goodwill to his now-allies in 1943, Stalin dissolved the Comintern; it was succeeded by the Communist Information Bureau (Cominform).

STALIN VERSUS TROTSKY

The Defeat of the Left Opposition

Prior to 1923 Leon Trotsky was seen by most Soviet citizens as one of the most prominent leaders of the Soviet Union. In 1917 he had led the Military Revolutionary Committee, which carried out the Bolshevik insurrection against the provisional government. He had negotiated the Treaty of Brest-Litovsk, had formed and led the Red Army to victory in the civil war, and was an important voice within the Soviet government concerning domestic and foreign affairs. To many, he seemed a natural successor to Lenin, whose health in 1923 took a sharp turn for the worse.

A NON-BOLSHEVIK BACKGROUND

However, Trotsky's enemies within the party were able to point to certain aspects of his past that made him seem "suspicious":

- Trotsky had opposed Lenin at the 1903 congress of the Russian Social-Democratic Workers' Party and had written a harsh polemic against him in "The Report of the Siberian Delegation." Lenin had replied in kind, and the two men were estranged until the summer of 1917.
- Trotsky was regarded by many party members as arrogant and out of touch with ordinary workers and peasants.
- Trotsky was Jewish, and there was a strain of anti-Semitism—often hidden but sometimes open—within both the party and the Soviet workers and peasants.

Trotsky himself did not take Stalin seriously as a political threat; he scorned him as merely a functionary of mediocre intelligence. He was far more preoccupied with opponents such as Bukharin and Zinoviev.

Lenin's Testament

In late 1922 and early 1923 Lenin, knowing his health was poor, wrote a short note to the party leadership, which was kept secret. In it, he evaluated the personalities of some of the top leaders, including Trotsky and Stalin:

> Comrade Stalin, having become Secretary-General, has unlimited authority concentrated in his hands, and I am not sure whether he will always be capable of using that authority with sufficient caution. Comrade Trotsky, on the other hand, as his struggles against the C.C. on the question of the People's Commissariat for Communications has already proved, is distinguished not only by outstanding ability. He is personally perhaps the most capable man in the present C.C., but he has displayed excessive self-assurance and shown excessive preoccupation with the purely administrative side of the work.
>
> These two qualities of the two outstanding leaders of the present C.C. can inadvertently lead to a split, and if our Party does not take steps to avert this, the split may come unexpectedly.

In a final note written shortly before his stroke Lenin recommended the removal of Stalin from his position as secretary-general of the party.

The note was read to the Political Committee, the central governing authority of the Communist Party, following Lenin's death in 1924, but for the sake of party unity those present, including Trotsky and Stalin, agreed to keep it secret.

By 1925 the party was embroiled in a full-scale faction fight between Trotsky, whose followers styled themselves the Left Opposition, and a triumvirate made up of Stalin, Zinoviev, and Lev Kamenev (1883–1936), another important party leader. Despite his best efforts, Trotsky found himself outmaneuvered by Stalin, who had full control of the party apparatus. The dispute took many forms, chiefly, in its early stages, regarding the degree to which the New Economic Policy should be continued. The Left Opposition called for putting reins on it, while the triumvirate advocated continuing it indefinitely.

By 1926 the triumvirate had broken apart, and Zinoviev and Kamenev had allied with Trotsky to form the United Opposition. Trotsky denounced Stalin, particularly over the latter's position on the situation in China. On Stalin's insistence the Chinese Communist Party offered an alliance with Chiang Kai-shek's Kuomintang, a bourgeois party. In 1927 Chiang Kai-shek turned on his erstwhile allies and massacred the communists in Shanghai.

EXPULSION AND EXILE

In late 1927 Trotsky and Zinoviev were expelled from the party. Trotsky was exiled, first to Kazakhstan and then to Turkey. Without their leader, the Left Opposition collapsed, and many of its members capitulated to the new regime.

Stalin was quick to consolidate his power. In the 1930s he launched a series of show trials, accusing prominent party members of treason and collaboration with the exiled Trotsky. By 1937 virtually all the members of the Bolshevik Central Committee at the time

of the revolution were dead, were in exile, or had been executed—
except for Stalin.

Trotsky in Exile

Despite his expulsion from the USSR, Trotsky continued to write and publish books and articles critical of Stalin and the Communist Party's policies. He himself was hounded from country to country (from Turkey to France, from France to Norway, and finally, in 1937, to Mexico). Trotsky lived in Mexico with his wife, Natalia Sedova, until 1940, when he was assassinated on Stalin's orders.

THE SOVIET UNION UNDER STALIN

Socialism in One Country

Before continuing, we need to examine the background of the man who, by the end of the 1930s, was the supreme ruler of the Soviet Union. Joseph Stalin (1878–1953) was the son of an alcoholic cobbler. Stalin enrolled in the Orthodox seminary to please his mother, who wanted him to be a priest. He was soon expelled for revolutionary activity and joined the political underground in the Caucasus, where he served more as an instigator of violent clashes than an organizer. In a party dominated by the self-proclaimed "bourgeois intelligentsia," he soon earned a reputation for a practical approach to revolution. (Lenin thought of him as a useful thug.) Once the Bolsheviks were in power, Stalin was the man who took care of the dull details of party and state administration.

The Man of Steel

Stalin wasn't Russian: he was born in the Caucasian province of Georgia. His original name was Iosif Dzhugashvili. Like Lenin, he used several aliases when he was active in the political underground. *Stalin* is from the Russian word for "steel," a good choice for a self-professed hard man.

Having control over the political machine helped Stalin triumph over his rivals in the power struggle that followed Lenin's death in 1924. Within four years he was the supreme Soviet leader.

STALINISM

The term *Stalinism* is used to describe a set of policies and a style of government rather than an ideology. Stalin would have been the first to declare that he was not a theory guy. He prided himself on adhering to the tenets of Marxist-Leninist ideology. Despite his protests, Stalin made two contributions to communist political theory that changed the shape of the Soviet state and its satellites: the theory that class struggle continues after the revolution, and the idea that socialist revolutions do not have to be international.

"Aggravation of the Class Struggle Along with the Development of Socialism"

According to Stalin, class struggle does not end with the revolution. In fact, the closer a society is to attaining a truly socialist state, the more the doomed remnants of the capitalist classes will struggle. Beginning in the 1930s Stalin used this theory to justify the repression of his political opponents, real and perceived, as counterrevolutionaries.

The Kirov Assassination

Many people opposed Stalin's methods, including party leader Sergei Kirov, who was assassinated in December 1934. Following Kirov's murder, Stalin launched a purge of alleged spies and counterrevolutionaries from the party, removing anyone who presented a threat to his authority. It is estimated that 500,000 people were executed and twelve million sent to the labor camps. Some historians suspect Stalin himself of having ordered Kirov's assassination as a way of getting rid of a rival and providing an excuse for the purge.

NOT ENOUGH

Lenin took the position that revolution in one country was not enough. In fact, he argued that because Russia was the weakest link in the industrialized world, revolution there would cause the entire capitalist-imperialist structure to fall. When it became clear that the socialist revolution was not going to spread into Western Europe, Stalin turned Lenin's dictum on its head and proclaimed "the proletariat can and must build the socialist society in one country."

The Growth of the Soviet Bloc

The USSR remained the only communist state until the end of World War II, when the Soviet Union installed left-wing governments in the countries of Eastern Europe that the Red Army had liberated from the Germans. These governments followed the Soviet pattern of a single-party system: substantial state ownership of the economy, adherence to an official ideology based on Marxism, and the maintenance of power through nondemocratic means.

CHINESE COMMUNISM

The East Is Red

Mao Zedong's idea of a peasant-based socialist revolution was an innovation in Marxist thinking, which held that the revolution would come from the urban poor. The idea of a peasant-based revolution was less startling in China, where dynasties often rose or fell as a result of peasant uprisings. In fact, it was a political truism that peasants are like water: they can float the boat or they can sink the boat.

MAOISM

According to the Chinese constitution, *Maoism* (called "Mao Zedong thought" in China) is simply "Marxism-Leninism defined in a Chinese context." Mao's most original contribution to Marxism was his recognition of Chinese peasants as the main force of revolution in China. As early as 1925, in his *Report on an Investigation of the Peasant Movement in Hunan*, he urged the Chinese Communist Party to turn its attention to the countryside. He argued that proletarianism was a mindset as much as an economic condition and that the Chinese peasants would be the "vanguard of the revolution."

Mao's *Little Red Book*

Very few people have read Marx's *Capital*, but millions of people have read a simplified version of Mao's political philosophy. *Quotations from Chairman Mao Zedong*, known in the West as *The Little Red Book*, was commissioned by General Lin Biao in 1964. Made up of selections from Mao's writings, the book was intended to simplify

Maoist thought for the relatively uneducated soldiers of the People's Liberation Army. Lin issued a free copy of the book to every soldier. It quickly became a vehicle for both spreading Maoist ideology and increasing literacy.

During the infamous Cultural Revolution in the 1960s and 1970s the book was made available to the public for the first time. Everyone in China soon owned a copy, and it became a talisman for members of the Red Guard.

THE CHINESE REVOLUTION BEGINS

In 1912 Dr. Sun Yat-sen's nationalist Revolutionary Alliance overthrew the Qing dynasty, which had ruled China since 1644. Sun became the provisional president of the Republic of China.

Sun Yat-sen

Both the People's Republic of China and Taiwan claim revolutionary leader Sun Yat-sen (1866–1925) as their founding father. Trained as a doctor in Hawaii, Sun returned to China to battle against the Qing dynasty, which he saw as the source of Chinese "backwardness." At first he envisioned establishing a constitutional monarchy but soon changed his goal to full democracy.

To make matters a bit more complicated, Sun and Chiang Kai-shek both married into the same family: the Soongs. Sun married Soong Ching-ling (1893–1981), while Chiang married Soong Mei-ling (1897–2003). While Mei-ling supported her husband and became a prominent voice in the China lobby in the United States, Ching-ling generally moved toward the communists, although she was not a member of the party.

The Republic didn't last long. In 1916 China's second president, Yuan Shikai, dissolved the new parliament and tried to make himself emperor. He was met with immediate opposition, via both political protests and military revolts in the provinces. Yuan died before he could consolidate his power. He left behind a conservative government seated in Beijing that claimed to rule all of China. In fact, the country was a mess of semi-independent warlords and armed political parties, most notably Sun Yat-sen's Kuomintang (Nationalist) Party.

THE BEGINNINGS OF CHINESE COMMUNISM

A new intelligentsia began to emerge at the end of the Qing dynasty as a result of educational reforms and the end of the centuries-old civil service examination system, which was based on history, poetry, and calligraphy. Thousands of young Chinese went to Japan, Europe, and the United States to study subjects that were not included in the classic Chinese curriculum: science, engineering, medicine, economics, law, and military science. They came to China with new academic knowledge and revolutionary ideas.

The New Culture Movement

The student leaders of the New Culture Movement, sometimes referred to as the Chinese Renaissance, called for "new thought" and "new literature" as they questioned Confucian values and institutions in the light of Western ideas. As a group, they were interested in national independence, individual liberties, and re-creating Chinese society and culture on modern terms.

The May Fourth Movement

On May 4, 1919, the news reached Beijing that the peacemakers at Versailles had decided to transfer the former German concessions in Shandong province to Japan instead of returning them to Chinese control. More than three thousand students demonstrated against the treaty provisions in Beijing's Tiananmen Square. Over the following weeks demonstrations against the Shandong provision spread beyond the students to the general population. Merchants closed their shops, workers went on strike, and banks suspended business.

Treaty Ports

In the nineteenth century the so-called Unequal Treaties between the Qing dynasty and various European governments opened "treaty ports" to foreign trade and habitation. Foreigners who lived in their own compounds in the treaty ports, called "concessions," did not have to pay Chinese taxes and were exempt from Chinese laws.

Faced with widespread demonstrations of anti-Japanese feeling, the Chinese government refused to sign the peace treaty.

Chinese Communist Party

The Chinese Communist Party grew directly out of the May Fourth Movement. The party's early leaders were professors and students who believed that China needed a social revolution.

Prior to 1905 the few Chinese socialists were students who had discovered Proudhon, Bakunin, and Kropotkin while studying in Paris and Tokyo. The attempted Russian revolution in 1905 excited interest among reform-minded Chinese, who saw parallels between the Qing dynasty and the Russian tsars. A translation of *The Communist Manifesto* into Chinese appeared in 1906, ending with a somewhat muted rendition of the original call to arms: "Then the world will be for the common people, and the sounds of happiness will reach the deepest springs. Ah! Come! People of every land, how can you not be roused?"

The Centrality of the Peasantry

The Chinese translator anticipated Mao's placement of peasants at the center of the Chinese revolution. In a note he explains that he used the phrase *common people* as the translation for *proletariat* since the Chinese word for "worker" did not include peasants.

After the initial flurry of excitement, Chinese radicals put Marxism to one side. After all, Marx himself had claimed that his cycle of historical development didn't apply to China.

The Russian Revolution of 1917 induced some Chinese intellectuals to look at Marx more closely. The most prominent among them was Li Dazhao (1889–1927), the head librarian of Beijing University. Excited by the possibilities of following the Russian example, Li created an informal study group that met at his office to discuss political developments and *Capital*. Six months later Chen Duxiu, then dean of the School of Letters at Beijing University, ran a special issue of *New Youth* devoted to Marxism, with Li Dazhao as the general editor. Soon radical study groups were meeting in a half dozen cities.

In May 1920 Chen Duxiu and Li Dazhao moved from studying Marxism to organizing. With the help of two agents from the Comintern, they founded a Soviet Youth League, laid plans for the creation of a communist party, and began recruiting. They soon had fifty members located throughout China and Japan.

In July 1921 Chen and Li held the founding meeting of the Chinese Communist Party (CCP) in Shanghai. Thirteen Chinese communists, including Mao Zedong, and two Comintern agents, attended it. Chen was elected to be the party's first secretary-general.

The CCP spent the next two years recruiting new members, publicizing Marxist ideology, publicizing the need for a national revolution directed against foreign imperialism, and attempting to organize China's handful of railway and industrial workers into unions.

By 1923 the party had almost three hundred members, and it was dangerous to be a known communist. With some arm-twisting on the part of the Comintern, the CCP became part of the Kuomintang.

MAO AND THE CHINESE REVOLUTION

The Great Helmsman

Mao Zedong (1893–1976) was the son of a wealthy peasant in Hunan province. His father wanted him to be a farmer and took him out of the local school when he was thirteen. Mao wanted more. Four years later he left home to study at the teacher's college in Hunan's provincial capital, where he became caught up in the revolution against the Qing dynasty in 1911.

In 1918 Mao finally graduated with his teaching certificate and went to Beijing to attend the university there. Like other graduate students, he had little money. He took a job as a library assistant to Li Dazhao, who introduced him to Marxism. Although Mao was one of the original members of the Chinese Communist Party, he did not become a party leader until the 1930s.

CIVIL WAR

After Sun Yat-sen's death in 1925, Chiang Kai-shek became the head of the Kuomintang. He immediately mobilized a massive campaign against the warlords in northern China. His intentions were to consolidate his power within the party and unify the country under his own leadership. In 1927, concerned about the rising influence of the Chinese Communist Party within the ranks of the Kuomintang, Chiang ordered the arrest and execution of hundreds of communists and other leftists.

Chiang Kai-shek

Unlike most of the Chinese revolutionaries, Chiang Kai-shek (1887–1975) trained as a career military officer. He served with the Japanese army from 1909 to 1911. While in Tokyo, he met young Chinese revolutionaries who converted him to republicanism. He fought in the revolt against the Qing dynasty and joined the Kuomintang in 1918.

The international community formally recognized Chiang's government after he conquered Beijing in 1928, but his hold on the country remained precarious. Northern warlords still challenged his authority. The Japanese invaded Manchuria in 1931, and showed signs of taking a large bite out of China's northern border. Closer to home the communists who had survived the 1927 purge created a Soviet-style republic in Jiangxi province, with its own army and government. Aided by a popular program of land redistribution, the Jiangxi Soviet controlled several million people by 1930.

Chiang decided to deal with the communist threat first. Between 1930 and 1934 he launched five campaigns against the Jiangxi Soviet. The communists successfully fought off the first four attacks using guerilla techniques that Mao designed.

Chiang brought in more forces for the fifth attack. In 1934 he built a series of concrete blockhouses around the communist positions manned with 700,000 troops. The communists might have succeeded in fending off the fifth attack if they had continued to use Mao's guerilla tactics. Unfortunately for them, the CCP's Central Committee had taken command of the communist forces when it moved to Jiangxi earlier that year. Instead of fighting a guerilla campaign, they met the larger and better-armed Kuomintang forces using more conventional military tactics.

The Long March

In October 1934, faced with defeat by Chiang's forces, the Red Army had only two options: surrender or retreat. They chose to retreat.

On October 16 the remaining 86,000 members of the Red Army, including administrative personnel and thirty women, broke through the Kuomintang line and began a 6,000-mile march from their base in southern China to the northwest province of Shanxi. The Long March took 368 days. For the first three months they suffered repeated Kuomintang attacks from the air and on the ground. They quickly ran out of rice and were reduced to eating first their horses and then their leather belts. Finally, they marched with empty stomachs. Only eight thousand survived the march.

By the time they reached Shanxi, Mao was the undisputed leader of the CCP. Other communist units in search of a leader soon joined them, raising their strength to thirty thousand.

The United Front

In 1937 Japan invaded China. Like squabbling siblings who quickly resolve their differences when an outsider picks on one of them, the Chinese Communist Party and the Kuomintang suspended hostilities and fought together against the Japanese.

The Sino-Japanese War gave the CCP a chance to revitalize itself. Operating out of their base in Shanxi, the communists used guerilla warfare tactics to harass the Japanese, often sending small units behind enemy lines to provide a nucleus for local resistance. In rural areas the communist fighters were often the only organized opposition to Japanese brutality. At the same time that they organized a willing population to supply food and hiding places for guerilla units, they also recruited new party members.

By the time Japan surrendered in 1945, popular opinion had shifted in favor of the communists. Disaffected Kuomintang troops joined Mao's army in large numbers, armed with captured Japanese weapons.

THE PEOPLE'S REPUBLIC OF CHINA

American efforts to build a coalition government between the two sides failed. Full-scale civil war broke out again in June 1946.

Despite American aid, Chiang's forces were on the run by late 1948. Beijing fell without a fight on January 31, 1949. The communist army took the Kuomintang capital of Nanking on April 23. Chiang Kai-shek and his supporters retreated to the island of Taiwan. On October 1 Chairman Mao announced the formation of the People's Republic of China, which he declared to be a "people's democratic dictatorship."

The CCP faced an enormous challenge. China had been torn by civil war for more than thirty years. With the brief exception of the Jiangxi Soviet, they had no experience in government. At first communist policies were based on what Mao later described as "copying from the Soviets." Ignoring his own policy of "encircling the cities from the countryside," Mao instituted a five-year plan focused on urban industrialization with Soviet technical assistance.

THE GREAT LEAP FORWARD AND THE CULTURAL REVOLUTION

Economic Disaster and Recovery

In 1956 Mao ignored the advice of key party members and initiated a campaign of "letting a hundred flowers bloom." Intellectuals were encouraged to speak out against abuses within the party.

To Mao's dismay, they did. For five weeks, from May 1 to June 7, people spoke out in closed party meetings and public rallies, in the official press and posters on city walls. They complained about harsh campaigns against counterrevolutionaries, the low standard of living, Soviet development models, censorship of foreign literature, and special privileges for CCP members. Students at the university in Beijing created a "Democratic Wall" covered with posters criticizing the CCP. Students began protest riots in cities across the country.

The backlash against the educated elite began in June. By the end of the year more than 300,000 intellectuals were branded "anticommunist, counterrevolutionary rightists." Many were sent to labor camps, imprisoned, or exiled to the countryside to experience life on the land. However, the campaign had significantly lowered Mao's prestige within the party. He now sought to recoup it.

THE GREAT LEAP FORWARD

In 1958 Mao introduced a three-year program, known as the Great Leap Forward, which was designed to increase production using labor rather than machines and capital expenditures. The capitalist model of industrialization was unacceptable for ideological reasons. The Soviet model of converting capital gained by the sale of agricultural products into heavy machinery was not viable: China's already large population meant there was no agricultural surplus to sell. Instead of slowly accumulating capital, Mao decided to leap forward by combining industrialization with collectivization.

The peasants were organized into large communes. Communal kitchens were established so women could be freed for agricultural work. Small "backyard furnaces" were set up in every village and urban neighborhood. Communes were given unreasonable goals for production and little guidance on how to achieve them. Productive agriculture ended almost overnight, as farm labor was diverted into small-scale industry.

Errors in implementing the program were made worse by a series of natural disasters, creating a large-scale famine. An estimated twenty million people died of starvation between 1959 and 1961, when the program was abandoned.

THE GREAT PROLETARIAN CULTURAL REVOLUTION

Following the failure of the Great Leap Forward, Mao began to denounce the development of "new bourgeois elements" among the party and technical elites in both the Soviet Union and China. Rather than a time of peacefully building the socialist state, he proclaimed that "protracted, complex, and sometimes even violent class struggle" would be constant elements of the revolution until the final stage of socialism was achieved.

In 1966 Mao announced a program that was officially intended to reaffirm the core values of Chinese communism and attack creeping bourgeois tendencies in the party bureaucracy: the Great Proletarian Cultural Revolution. Its unofficial purpose was to purge the party leadership of anyone who opposed him.

Mao closed schools and invited student groups to join paramilitary Red Guard units. Working under the slogan "fight selfishness, criticize revisionism," the Red Guard burned books, destroyed Confucian and Buddhist temples, and hunted down "counterrevolutionaries." Revisionists, intellectuals, and anyone suspected of "ideological weakness" (code for disagreeing with Mao) were all fair targets. Some were punished with nothing worse than wearing a dunce cap and publicly confessing their errors. Others were beaten, tortured, killed, or driven to commit suicide. Urban residents, intellectuals, and government officials were relocated to the country to "learn from the peasants." The worst of the Cultural Revolution ended with Mao's death in 1976.

The Legacy of the Cultural Revolution

China continues to grapple with the impact of the Cultural Revolution on its society. Much of the worst artistic destruction took place in and around Beijing, but many people were caught up in vicious "criticism and self-criticism" campaigns. Those who were not killed or permanently injured were psychologically scarred, in most cases for life.

WORLD WAR II

The USSR Fights for Its Life

In the early 1930s many people viewed with alarm the rise of fascism in Italy and Germany. Adolf Hitler (1889–1945) embodied the spirit of militarism and intolerance that swept across Europe. Among the first victims of his government were members of the German Socialist Party and the German Communist Party, who were summarily committed to concentration camps, along with union leaders and other dissenters.

Hitler made no secret of his overall aims: the expansion of living space for the German people, especially to the east, and the destruction of the Jews, whom Hitler viewed as responsible for all the troubles that had befallen Germany.

The Soviet government had a more ambiguous position toward Germany, with whom it shared a border. As German demands on neighboring states increased, Stalin sought a temporary alliance with Britain and France. Neither state was interested, however, and in August 1939, in a move that shocked his followers around the world, Stalin agreed to a non-aggression pact with the Nazi regime.

Despite the non-aggression pact, Hitler's long-range plans in no way changed. In the spring of 1941, with France conquered and Britain seemingly helpless, he began plans for an invasion of the Soviet Union.

On June 22, 1941, German forces struck across the border, deep into the USSR. Although Stalin had been warned of the impending invasion by many sources, including the British government and the Soviet intelligence services, he refused to believe them. As a result, the Soviet forces were woefully underprepared, and the Nazi armies advanced rapidly toward Moscow, Leningrad (St. Petersburg), and elsewhere. Fortunately for the USSR, Hitler was overconfident, predicting such a quick end to the war that he would not permit generals to order soldiers to bring along winter clothing. Therefore, when the German armies became stuck outside Moscow and Leningrad and the Russian winter advanced, the German troops suffered and fell back in the face of Soviet counteroffensives.

About-Face Overnight

Since the negotiations between Germany and the Soviet Union had been kept largely secret, the news of the pact caught communist parties outside the USSR almost entirely by surprise. Prior to the pact they had denounced German fascism vigorously. Overnight, that changed with no explanation. George Orwell satirized this in his novel *Nineteen Eighty-Four*: Oceania is at war with Eurasia and allied with Eastasia when, in the middle of a political rally, everything changes and Oceania is suddenly at war with Eastasia and allied with Eurasia. Any inconsistencies are set down to unnamed "saboteurs."

The turning point of the war came in 1942 in the city of Stalingrad. Hitler regarded the city as key to his military plans, since if Germany took it, the Nazis would have access to the extensive oil wells of the Caucasus. However, the Germans were unable to take the city by siege. Once again, the Russian winter came to the aid of the country's defenders, and in 1943 the Germans were themselves surrounded by a Soviet army. In January the German commander surrendered, and the Soviets began pushing back the German armies.

By April 1945 Soviet armies had penetrated all the way to Berlin. On April 30 Hitler committed suicide, and Germany surrendered a week later.

AFTERMATH

Despite its victory in the war, the Soviet Union had suffered horribly. About twenty-seven million Soviet citizens died, of whom nineteen million were civilians. Industry and agriculture were wrecked and took decades to rebuild. Occupants of Moscow and Leningrad had starved during the long siege of their cities, some resorting to cannibalism.

Returning POWs

Tragically, Stalin's paranoia, which had by then reached epic proportions, left him convinced that the Soviets who had surrendered to German forces during the war were traitors. When the POWs were liberated from the horrendous camps in which they had been held, they were arbitrarily sent to other camps in Siberia, where many of them perished.

Despite the horrors of the war, the highly controlled economy of the Soviet Union enabled the country to make a relatively rapid recovery. Stalin used the war as an opportunity to extend Soviet influence to a number of Eastern European nations, which nationalized large parts of their economies and became part of the newly formed Soviet bloc. The stage was set for the opening of a new war— one that would be fought less with bombs and bullets and more with propaganda and espionage: the Cold War.

THE COLD WAR

The Iron Curtain Comes Down

In March 1946 former British prime minister Winston Churchill gave a speech in Fulton, Missouri. In it, he said:

> From Stettin in the Baltic to Trieste in the Adriatic an iron curtain has descended across the Continent. Behind that line lie all the capitals of the ancient states of Central and Eastern Europe. Warsaw, Berlin, Prague, Vienna, Budapest, Belgrade, Bucharest, and Sofia; all these famous cities and the populations around them lie in what I must call the Soviet sphere, and all are subject, in one form or another, not only to Soviet influence but to a very high and in some cases increasing measure of control from Moscow.

Many historians view Churchill's "iron curtain" speech as the beginning of the Cold War, a period that lasted from the end of World War II until 1989 and the collapse of the Soviet Union.

BERLIN

The curtain divided many countries from one another, but nowhere was its impact felt more dramatically than in the city of Berlin.

After the end of the war, with much of the city in ruins, the Allies agreed to divide it into four sectors: Soviet, American, British, and French. Stalin's plans were to make the entire city of Berlin, and eventually all of Germany, into a socialist state. However, by 1947 the US, Britain, and France had begun to consolidate their zones of influence in Germany into an entity that would eventually be called West Germany. Stalin and the German communists responded by stepping up pressure on Berlin, which lay well within the Soviet zone. The Western powers responded by airlifting supplies to the non-Soviet sectors of Berlin. The airlift continued for almost a year, from the middle of 1948 to September 1949 (the Soviets lifted their blockade in May), at which point other supply routes into the city were established. As the airlift made clear, though, for the foreseeable future Berlin would remain a divided city.

The Berlin Wall

Throughout the 1950s East Germany made various attempts to control the movement of its population, particularly to restrict emigration to West Germany. These proved ineffective, and in 1961 the East German government began construction of a wall, closing off East Berlin from the West. It ran for more than 96 miles, and over the course of its existence it was expanded and remodeled several times.

"Ich bin ein Berliner!"

In one of the most famous speeches of his presidency, John F. Kennedy, visiting Berlin in June 1963, declared:

> Two thousand years ago, the proudest boast was *civis romanus sum* ["I am a Roman citizen"]. Today, in the world of freedom, the proudest boast is *Ich bin ein Berliner!* ["I am a citizen of Berlin!"]

The wall became a visible symbol of the Cold War. There were various attempts by East Germans to cross it, despite the presence of heavily armed guards and watchtowers. There were official crossing points, and it was possible for West Berliners to visit the eastern part of the city, although this was highly restricted.

It is estimated that about five thousand people crossed the wall successful and illegally. How many died trying isn't clear; the number may have been as high as two hundred.

The Wall Comes Down

As the power of the Soviet state and its bloc began to crumble in 1989, pressure increased on the East German government to allow greater travel to the West. Many people left East Germany and traveled to West Berlin or other parts of West Germany. People gathered at the wall and demanded that the government let them through. Finally, on the evening of November 9, 1989, people began hacking at the wall with pickaxes, shovels, and anything else that came to hand. Soldiers declined to fire on the crowds as the demolition continued.

The destruction of the hated wall symbolized the beginning of the end of the Cold War between the socialist East and the capitalist West.

The Wall Today

Although much of the wall was demolished and the two halves of Germany were reunited in a single nation, sections of the wall remain today as monuments to the memory of the Cold War. Many of the segments still standing are covered with the graffiti that adorned the wall when it stood as a barrier to free travel.

ALTERNATIVES TO STALINISM

The Third Way

Despite Stalin and Stalinism's iron grip on much of the communist world, there were some significant dissensions from his views. The most prominent of these was the course held by the Yugoslav leader Josip Broz Tito (1892–1980). His approach to domestic and international affairs, generally more liberal than that of his Soviet counterpart, was often characterized as the "third way"—that is, a socialism that was different from the anti-communism of many socialist leaders but at the same time was not the repressive force that governed the Soviet Union.

TITO

Josip Broz Tito was born in 1892 in what is now Croatia. He became interested in socialism when quite young and became active in the Social Democratic Party of Croatia and Slavonia. Yugoslavia fought on the side of Germany and Austro-Hungary in the First World War, and Tito enlisted in the army and fought in several battles. He was wounded and captured by the Russians and eventually transferred to labor duty in St. Petersburg in 1917.

Comrades and Lovers

While fighting in Siberia, Tito met a fourteen-year-old girl who hid him from the Whites and nursed him back to health. The following year he married her, and together they traveled to Yugoslavia.

It was a life-changing event. He arrived in July, when demonstrations and meetings led by the Bolsheviks were everyday events. After taking part in several of these, Tito was arrested by the provisional government. On his way to exile, he escaped, then traveled to Siberia to evade the authorities.

There he was recruited by elements of the Red Guard to help fight in the nascent civil war against the White armies. He did so and eventually, in 1920, returned to Yugoslavia, a fully committed communist.

Although Tito worked various jobs, by the 1930s he was a full-time professional revolutionary. He served time in prison for his activities, but this did not deter him. In 1939 he became acting secretary of the Communist Party of the Soviet Union. Despite rumors of Trotskyist sympathies that swirled around him, he managed to avoid arrest even while living in Moscow.

TITO IN WORLD WAR II

In 1941 German armies invaded Yugoslavia, and the government fled. Tito returned to his country on orders from the USSR and formed a group of partisan fighters. They were officially recognized by the Allies, and in 1944 the exiled king, Peter, called on all Yugoslavs to support them. In 1945, with the fall of the Axis, Tito organized a new government with himself as its head.

Why Was Yugoslavia Different?

Unlike other USSR satellite states, Yugoslavia liberated itself from Nazi rule through its own military efforts. This gave Tito a degree of independence from Stalin and created the basis for a split.

From the beginning it was clear that Yugoslavia would follow a different socialist path than the USSR. Tito wrote, "We study and take as an example the Soviet system, but we are developing socialism in our country in somewhat different forms." Thus provoked, Stalin began plotting a full-scale invasion of Yugoslavia, which was expelled from the Cominform. "I will shake my little finger and there will be no more Tito," Stalin declared. However, the planned invasion never occurred.

Instead, having been pushed out of the Cominform, Tito's government began receiving aid from the United States. Tito was careful to make no conditions for receiving the aid, but he was able to differentiate himself from the Stalinist regime. Matters were helped by Stalin's death in 1953, after which the Yugoslav government also started receiving aid again from the Cominform.

Tito, in this way, was able to occupy a position in the Cold War between the Soviet bloc and the West. In 1950 his government eased the management of state-run businesses and allowed a limited measure of workplace democracy and profit sharing.

The Non-Aligned Movement

In 1961 Tito, along with leaders of Egypt, India, Indonesia, and Ghana, formed the Non-Aligned Movement, a group of countries that attempted to maneuver between the two superpowers while strengthening their ties to the underdeveloped world. One result was that Yugoslavia had a far more liberal travel policy than Soviet bloc countries, something that allowed significant exchanges of scientific, cultural, and economic information. Thus, Yugoslavia in the 1950s and 1960s was an important international example of a "third way," one lying between the rigid socialist dogma of Stalinism and the capitalist West.

THE FRANKFURT SCHOOL AND ANTONIO GRAMSCI

"Cultural Marxism"

In addition to its political and economic aspects, socialism has had a wide cultural impact on modern thinking. Many conservative commentators have even accused higher education in the United States and elsewhere of being permeated with "cultural Marxism." They place the blame for this largely on one person and one institution: the Italian communist Antonio Gramsci and the research institute commonly referred to as the Frankfurt School.

ANTONIO GRAMSCI

Antonio Gramsci (1891–1937) was a leader of the Italian Communist Party, although his most important work was done behind bars. After some years of activity in union struggles in Turin, he became a founder and the leader of the Italian Communist Party. However, he was imprisoned by Mussolini's government in 1926 and spent the next decade in prison. This was particularly difficult for him because since childhood he had suffered from a variety of medical conditions. He was hunchbacked, probably due to a childhood accident, had a weak heart, and had recurring tuberculosis. In prison his health problems were exacerbated, and by the time he was released from a prison clinic he had only days to live.

Stopping the Brain

The officials who ordered Gramsci's arrest were aware of his importance in the socialist movement in Italy. In his final speech at Gramsci's trial the prosecutor thundered, "We must stop this brain from working for twenty years!" Sadly, Gramsci did not last even that long.

The Prison Notebooks

While in prison Gramsci struggled to work out a comprehensive theory of Marxism and culture. This was challenging, since very little had previously been written on the subject. Gramsci filled notebook after notebook with jottings, thoughts, and essays. The result was a complex and at times confusing set of ideas.

Coded Language

Understanding Gramsci's thoughts is made more difficult by the fact that his notebooks were subject to prison examination and censorship. Gramsci was thus forced to use code words for various concepts. Fortunately, edited and annotated versions of the notebooks have been published, making their study much easier.

Cultural Hegemony

One of Gramsci's central ideas is that social systems such as capitalism retain power not just through force exercised by the state but also by developing a set of ideas and cultural practices that, over time, become normalized. Gramsci thus distinguished between "political society"—meaning the part of the state that exercises physical control over the populace (the armed forces, police, and so forth)—and "civil society," meaning those institutions, primarily educational, that produce the ideology that is accepted by everyone as the basis of society. In this he assigns an important role to intellectuals. Capitalism, he argues, has produced a set of intellectuals who justify its existence. The struggle to create a socialist society, therefore, takes place on two levels: the political and the intellectual. Socialists must create their own cultural norms that, over time, will conquer and replace the cultural hegemony of capitalism.

Economic Determinism

Given his views on cultural hegemony and the importance of ideas in social struggle, it's perhaps unsurprising that Gramsci resisted what he saw as the economic determinism of traditional Marxism. An overreliance on economics and a purely economic understanding of society would lead one to miss the equally important cultural factors. Gramsci viewed the Marxism expounded by the Communist Party in the Soviet Union as crude, but he generally downplayed this criticism in his notebooks.

Rediscovery

Gramsci remained a relatively obscure thinker until the 1970s. By that time excerpts from the prison notebooks had been published and translated into many languages. Volumes had also been published containing his letters from prison, his political writings from before his imprisonment, and a number of biographies and commentaries. As a result, Gramscian studies are very much alive today, and he is regarded as one of the most important thinkers of twentieth-century socialism.

THE FRANKFURT SCHOOL

The Frankfurt School refers to a group of intellectuals associated with the Institute for Social Research, a group affiliated with Goethe University Frankfurt. Although many of its members were exiled from Germany during World War II, it continued to function, largely in America, where many of its members had fled.

Although there were a good many differences between them, virtually all those who were part of the Frankfurt School considered themselves socialists. Most thought of themselves as Marxists, albeit extremely unorthodox ones. Generally they had no affiliation with political parties, preferring to operate in the realm of pure theory. Insofar as they had an approach to socialist issues, they attempted to find a synthesis between Marx, Freud, and other elements of Modernism. The end result was called Critical Theory, although its parameters remained somewhat hazy.

Adorno and Horkheimer

The two principal leaders of the Institute during its first few decades were music critic Theodor Adorno (1903–1969) and sociologist Max Horkheimer (1895–1973). Together they produced a body of work including *Dialectic of Enlightenment*, the most complete exposition of the Frankfurt School's thought.

Their theory was essentially pessimistic—not surprising since it was written in the shadow of Hitler's rise to power. They argued that the Enlightenment, far from being a source of political advance, became the underlying theory of totalitarianism in the twentieth century. They believed that modern culture had essentially become an "industry" to mass produce cultural goods with the purpose of lulling the masses into security.

Radio

Adorno and Horkheimer lived in an age in which mass communication was just becoming possible through radio. Others, including Roosevelt in the United States and Hitler in Germany, took advantage of this fact and used it to their advantage. After that, of course, mass communication spread, first through television and then, in the age of the Internet, through social media.

THE BROADER IMPACT OF THE SCHOOL

Other members of the Frankfurt School had a significant impact on modern cultural thinking. These included Eric Fromm, whose work dealt primarily with psychology; Franz Neumann, whose book *Behemoth* marked a significant high point in the study of fascism in Germany; Friedrich Pollock, who examined the USSR's attempts to create a planned socialist economy; and others.

Herbert Marcuse

Among the most influential members of the Frankfurt School was Herbert Marcuse (1898–1979), who came to the United States after the rise of Hitler. Marcuse worked at a number of different schools, winding up at the University of California, San Diego. During the last decade of his life he became a leading influence on the New Left in the United States, largely as a result of his book *One-Dimensional Man*. In it, Marcuse argued that the Western working class had largely lost its revolutionary potential, and that this potential now lay with young people, especially students—a viewpoint highly appealing to the leaders of the student-based New Left. It was said in some leftist circles, especially in California, that revolutionaries needed to study the three Ms: Marx, Mao, and Marcuse.

Marcuse's Major Works

Marcuse was the member of the Frankfurt School who offered the most systematic study of Freud and attempted to fuse Freud and Marx in *Eros and Civilization*. He also authored an important study of Hegel's relationship to Marx, *Reason and Revolution*.

Following the end of the war most of the leaders of the Institute returned to Germany and continued their work. The most significant leader of this socialist tendency in recent years has been Jürgen Habermas, a sociologist whose ideas, in the views of many, have diverged very far from the original leaders of the Frankfurt School.

Walter Benjamin

One of the most interesting and complex of the figures associated with the Frankfurt School was Walter Benjamin (1892–1940), who didn't fit into any of the categories associated with the school but was nonetheless part of it. He wrote on a vast number of subjects, but his masterwork, *The Arcades Project*, remained uncompleted at his death. He believed that in the study of Parisian life in the nineteenth century he had found a subject that could support a socialist cultural criticism. When the Nazis rose to power, he fled from Germany to France; when German troops marched into France, he and others tried to escape over the Pyrenees into neutral Spain. He was stopped at the Spanish border, and in despair he committed suicide.

UTOPIAN SOCIALIST MOVEMENTS IN BRITAIN

Luddites and Chartism

Even though Karl Marx spent the most productive years of his career studying in the British Library, he had little influence on the development of British socialism. Unlike their European counterparts, British socialists drew their inspiration from a homegrown radical tradition built on religious nonconformity, the concept of British liberties, and Robert Owen's Cooperative Movement. Whether based on labor, economics, or an outraged sense of beauty, British socialism leaned toward reform rather than revolution.

CHARTISM: THE FIRST MASS WORKING-CLASS MOVEMENT

Chartism was a movement for parliamentary reform that grew out of working-class protests against the economic injustices caused by the Industrial Revolution. In 1815 the passage of the Corn Laws made it clear to working-class radicals that the people who controlled Parliament made laws that primarily benefited themselves. It was a classic Catch-22. The only way the working classes could improve the conditions under which they worked was to get the vote so they could send their own representatives to Parliament. In order to get the vote, they had to change the laws.

The Chartist movement was named after the People's Charter, drafted by London radical William Lovett in May 1838. The Charter contained six demands for political change:

1. Universal manhood suffrage
2. Equally populated electoral districts
3. Vote by secret ballot
4. Annually elected Parliaments
5. Payment of stipends to members of Parliament
6. Abolition of property qualifications for members of Parliament

When the Charter was first distributed to popular groups for discussion, many radicals dismissed it as too moderate, but it clearly fired the popular imagination. All over the country working-class institutions of all types—trade unions, educational societies, and radical associations—transformed themselves into Chartist centers.

Equal Populations in Voting Districts

Population growth, internal migration, and new industrial cities meant parliamentary representation no longer reflected population distribution. Growing cities, like Manchester, had no representatives, while boroughs with declining populations had two. The most notorious of the "rotten boroughs" was Old Sarum, which had a representative but no town.

Taking the slogan "Political power our means, social happiness our end," the first Chartist convention met in London in February 1839, to prepare a petition to present to Parliament. Their leaders were arrested, and leadership shifted to the more radical element of the movement. In November a group of "physical force" Chartists staged an armed uprising at Newport. It was quickly suppressed. While the majority of the Chartists concentrated on petitioning for the Newport leaders to be released from jail, others led small uprisings in Sheffield, East London, and Bradford. The principal leaders were transported to the penal colony in Australia. Other Chartist leaders were arrested and served short jail sentences.

The Power of Moral Force

The original leaders of the Chartist movement had no interest in violence, preferring to rely on "moral force" to persuade Parliament to accept the Charter. Others, known as "physical force" Chartists, reserved the possibility of force as an alternative means of persuasion.

The first stage of the Chartist movement was a loose federation of working-class organizations held together by a common goal. With many of the original leaders in jail, a second generation came forward who had a new emphasis on efficient organization and moderate tactics. Using skills learned in the trade union movement, they formed the National Charter Association of Great Britain, complete with constitution, quarterly dues, and membership cards. Under their leadership, Chartists collected more than three million signatures on a second petition, which they presented in 1842. Parliament paid no more attention to the second petition than it had to the first.

The last great burst of Chartism appeared in 1848: Britain's response to the "Hungry Forties." On April 10 a new Chartist convention held a mass meeting in Kennington Common in preparation for a march to present yet another petition to Parliament. The army refused to allow the procession to cross the Thames, forcing the leaders to deliver the document in a hansom cab. The petition itself had only 1.9 million signatures, including presumed forgeries from Queen Victoria and Mr. Punch of Punch and Judy, a popular puppet show. Even the Queen's signature wasn't enough; Parliament ignored the Charter for a third time.

The Charter Lives On

The Chartist movement died, but the ideas behind it did not. Between 1858 and 1918 Parliament adopted five of the six points of the Charter. The only point that was never adopted was the annual election of Parliament; presumably members of Parliament couldn't face the idea of annual campaigning.

CHRISTIAN SOCIALISM

The Christian socialism movement began shortly after the failure of the final Chartist effort in April 1848. In many ways, Christian socialism was the flip-side of Chartism: a largely middle-class movement that attempted to ameliorate the problems caused by the Industrial Revolution by applying the social principles of Christianity to modern industrial life.

The main force behind the movement was Anglican theologian Frederick Denison Maurice (1805–1872). In 1838 Maurice laid out the central principles of Christian socialism in *The Kingdom of Christ*. He proclaimed "socialism's true character as the great Christian revolution of the nineteenth century." He argued that the competition that lies at the heart of capitalism is fundamentally un-Christian and the source of society's ills. The answer was to replace competition with cooperation.

In practical terms Christian socialism meant the creation of Owenite cooperative societies, which Maurice saw as a modern application of the communal tradition of early Christianity. Christian socialists joined forces with the cooperative movement and founded several small cooperative societies that promoted co-partnerships and profit sharing in industry. The longest lasting of the movement's social experiments was the formation of the Working Men's College in London in 1854.

The Opiate of the People

Christian socialists occasionally took positions that upset more conservative Christians. Four years after Marx declared that religion was the opiate of the people, the most well-known Christian socialist, novelist Charles Kingsley, warned readers in *Politics for the People* that the Bible was used as an "opium-dose for keeping beasts of burden patient while they were being overloaded."

The original adherents of Christian socialism drifted away from the movement in the late 1850s. The 1880s saw a more formal revival of the movement, with different denominations founding officially sanctioned Christian socialist groups.

WILLIAM MORRIS

Poet and craftsman William Morris (1834–1896) is best known today for his wallpaper designs and his often-quoted dictum that a person should have nothing in his home that he does "not know to be useful or believe to be beautiful." Long before he made his way to socialism, Morris began what he described as a "campaign against the age," rejecting the commercial, industrial, and scientific society of his time for its visual squalor and social complacency. Part of the Pre-Raphaelite Brotherhood, with its romantic yearnings for the medieval, Morris designed wallpaper, textiles, rugs, and furniture. Morris's design company was originally an artistic cooperative with seven members who led the international design revival known as the Arts and Crafts movement. The company served as a pattern for Morris's vision of small artisanal studios as the economic base for society.

Morris came to socialism through his belief that without dignified, creative work, people become disconnected from life. Building on Thomas Carlyle's *Past and Present* (1843) and John Ruskin's *The Stones of Venice* (1851–1853), Morris looked at bleak industrial cities and an impoverished proletariat and questioned whether either constituted real progress.

As a socialist, Morris rejected industrialism and capitalism because they degraded human beings and undervalued craftsmanship. The transition from workshop to factory meant that men were put to work making shoddy goods and needless gadgets. Morris wanted mankind to find fulfillment in the production of beautiful objects. His version of socialism was intended to liberate the average man from drudgery and restore beauty to his life.

Morris envisioned an alternative society in which everyone had equal opportunities for education. The division of labor that stands at the heart of factory work would be restricted so that the work of artists and craftsmen would be valued. He emphasized the importance of returning to small artisanal production and the right of all members of society to find joy and self-expression in work.

Morris and Organized Socialism

Morris came to organized socialism late. In the 1870s he became increasingly disturbed by what he believed were the related issues of Britain's class divisions and apathy toward art. He tackled the question of art first, cofounding an early conservation group, the Society for the Protection of Ancient Buildings, and giving hundreds of public lectures on the relationship between a country's aesthetic standards and its social conditions.

In 1883, at the age of forty-nine, Morris joined the Social Democratic Federation, a revolutionary socialist party with Marxist roots. The Federation soon divided over the question of involvement in parliamentary politics. In 1884 Morris found himself the unwilling leader of the Socialist League, a breakaway group that stood against political action.

Morris remained active in the socialist movement until the 1890s, when his health began to fail and internal dissentions divided the Socialist League.

The New Age

Morris's work profoundly influenced a group of architects, artists, and intellectuals associated with the progressive newspaper *The New Age*, between 1907 and 1920. Under the leadership of Alfred Richard Orage, *The New Age* was the early twentieth-century paper for alternative thinkers. Dissatisfied with Fabian socialism, Orage searched instead for a basic "re-evaluation of values." Demanding political and economic rights for man was only the first step. As far as Orage himself was concerned, the search for new values meant an "ethical and spiritual rejection of capitalism and its vision of progress," based on his reading of Carlyle, Ruskin, Morris, and Marx.

Seeking a third path between capitalism and socialism, the paper published attacks on modern industrial society from both the right and the left: anarchists, Jacobites, medieval revivalists, and land reformers. The magazine's best-known contributors were Hilaire Belloc, G.K. Chesterton, and Ezra Pound.

THE FABIAN SOCIETY

Economist and historian Sidney Webb coined the phrase "the inevitability of gradualness" to describe the Fabian Society's approach to socialism. Founded in 1884, the Fabian Society believed that the transformation of British society from capitalism to socialism could be best achieved through what Sidney Webb described as "permeation" of the nation's intellectual and political life. Although they agreed with Marx that this transformation was inevitable, they disagreed about the process. The Fabians believed that the transformation of society would be gradual and experimental, the result of parliamentary reforms rather than revolution.

The Delayer

The Fabian Society took its name from Roman general Quintus Fabius Maximus Verrucosus Cunctator, who earned the nickname "Fabius the Delayer" during the Punic Wars, when his tactics of avoiding pitched battles allowed him to wear down, and ultimately defeat, the stronger Carthaginian forces.

The ultimate goal for society, outlined by Beatrice Webb in the *Minority Report of the Poor Law Commission* (1909), was a democratically elected, centralized socialist state that would guarantee its citizens a "national minimum standard of civilized life." The Fabians envisioned the establishment of public enterprises at the local, regional, and state levels, which would be financed by taxes on rent, as defined by David Ricardo. Since these public enterprises would be funded through taxes, they would not be burdened with some of the expenses common to private enterprises and could therefore offer better wages and working conditions. The Fabians also proposed that public utilities, common carriers, and businesses that were already under the control of private monopolies should be nationalized.

For the most part the Fabians were middle-class intellectuals, led by Sidney and Beatrice Webb and playwright George Bernard Shaw. The society's membership was never large: only 8,400 at its height in 1946.

The LSE

The London School of Economics and Political Science (LSE) was founded in 1895 by the Fabian Society for the purpose of creating a better society through the study of poverty issues. In the early twentieth century the school became a training ground for leaders of the underdeveloped world.

Rather than founding a political party, the Fabians preferred to influence existing parties. In 1900 the Fabians helped organize the Labour Representation Committee, which became the Labour Party in 1906.

THE BRITISH LABOUR PARTY

A Party of Its Own

Scottish socialist Keir Hardie (1856–1915) became a symbol of the working class in Victorian England, his famous cloth cap the antithesis of the top hat worn by members of the privileged classes. Born James Kerr, Hardie was the illegitimate son of a farm maidservant and a ship's carpenter. His father was an early trade unionist.

Hardie went to work when he was seven or eight. When he was eleven, he took a job in the local mines as a trapper, working the airshaft traps that ventilated the mines. He worked as a coal miner for the next eleven years.

Hardie's Education

Like many working-class radicals, Hardie was largely self-taught. With little formal education, he was well read in history and literature. Later in life he claimed he was particularly influenced by Thomas Carlyle's satirical novel *Sartor Resartus* (first published serially in *Fraser's Magazine* in 1833 and 1834). In addition to reading widely, he taught himself to write Pitman's shorthand.

In 1878 Hardie left the mines to become active in the trade union movement. At first he opened a small shop in Glasgow and wrote articles for a paper there. Beginning in 1881 he was involved in the effort to organize a miners' union, moving from county to county as he established local chapters. For several years he cobbled together a living, supplementing his salary as corresponding secretary for different union chapters with various part-time jobs.

In 1886, with the Ayrshire Union stable enough to pay him a full-time salary, Hardie began to shift his interest to politics and socialism. He threw himself into politics with the same fervor he showed as a union organizer. He founded two monthly journals, the short-lived *The Miner*, which advocated a Scottish miner's federation, and the more widely based *The Labor Leader*; served as operating secretary for the short-lived Glasgow Labour Party; and attended the inaugural congress of the Second International in Paris in 1889, educating himself by attending both Marxist and non-Marxist sessions.

In 1888 Hardie ran for Parliament for the first time as an independent labor candidate. He received only 617 votes but caught the attention of the Liberal political machine. In 1891 the Liberal Party offered him the candidacy for West Ham South in London, a working-class neighborhood with a heavy union presence.

Hardie's first term in Parliament was not a success. He lost his seat in the 1895 elections. He ran again, without success, in 1896 and 1900.

Parliamentary Elections

In Great Britain parliamentary elections are not held on a fixed cycle. Sessions of Parliament cannot last more than five years, but the sovereign may dissolve a session of Parliament at any time after consulting with the prime minister. Sessions are dissolved for a variety of reasons, including the inability to maintain a working coalition in the House of Commons.

Even though he was losing at the polls, Hardie was building a strong political foundation for the future. Rather than relying on loose alliances with the Liberal Party, he founded the Independent Labour Party (ILP) in 1893, with the basic strategy of creating an alliance between the trade unions and the socialist societies. In 1894 he began to publish *The Labor Leader* every week rather than once a month, giving himself a platform for his positions.

A NEW PARTY

In February 1900 Hardie's Independent Labour Party joined with other labor and socialist groups, including the Trades Union Congress and the Fabian Society, to form the Labour Representation Committee (LRC). A forerunner of the Labour Party, the LRC was organized to promote the election of working-class candidates to Parliament. In 1906 the LRC turned itself into the Labour Party and won twenty-nine seats in Parliament in the general election. Hardie was elected member of Parliament for Merthyr Tydfil in South Wales.

By the end of World War I the Labour Party had a solid membership base, thanks to two important changes in the political climate:

- A substantial growth in the number of trade union members.
- The Representation of the People Act of 1918, which extended the vote to all men over twenty-one and gave the vote for the first time to women over thirty who met a property qualification.

In 1918 the Labour Party officially proclaimed itself a socialist party and unveiled a new reform program, *Labour and the New Social Order*, drafted by Fabian Society leaders Sidney and Beatrice Webb. The party's new goals included full employment with a minimum wage and a maximum workweek, public ownership of industry, progressive taxation, and the expansion of education and social service.

By 1922 the Labour Party had replaced the Liberals as the official opposition party. In 1924 Britain elected its first Labour government.

CREATION OF THE WELFARE STATE

British Social Engineers

The one-two punch of the Great Depression and World War II left Western Europe ready for a change. Economies and societies needed to be rebuilt. In an overwhelming rejection of the free-market economy and the parties that supported it, Western Europe voted Left. Britain, Norway, and Sweden elected socialist governments. Socialist parties helped form coalition governments in Holland, Denmark, Switzerland, Austria, Belgium, Italy, and France. For the first time socialist parties were in power in virtually all of Western Europe.

THE ROOTS OF THE WELFARE STATE

The Russian Revolution left a clear divide between parties that described themselves as socialist and those that described themselves as communist. In 1945 Western Europe's socialist parties were the heirs of Eduard Bernstein and the Fabians, not those of Marx and Lenin. Although they retained an ideological commitment to the creation of a socialist state, they abandoned revolution in favor of reform before they took power. Elected to office with a clear mandate for change, Europe's socialist parties developed variations of "welfare socialism," all of which included a range of social welfare programs and a reformed capitalist structure regulated by the state.

In fact, post-war socialist parties weren't the first to set up social welfare programs. In a move intended to win the allegiance of the working classes away from the socialists, Chancellor Otto van Bismarck set up the first compulsory national social insurance programs in Germany, including a health insurance plan in 1893, workers' compensation in 1894, and general pensions for the elderly and the disabled in 1889. Austria and Hungary soon followed Germany's example. Conscious of the new Labour Party breathing down its neck, Herbert Asquith's Liberal government instituted a similar series of reforms in Britain in 1911, including Britain's first health and unemployment insurance plans, old-age pensions, a national network of labor exchanges, and trade boards with the power to set minimum wages for their industries.

Social Market Economy

The German Social Democratic Party, reconstructed after its demise at the hands of the Nazis, dropped its commitment to Marxism in its 1959 Bad Godesberg program. The party replaced Marxism with the pursuit of a "social market economy" that would include "as much competition as possible—as much planning as necessary."

CLEMENT ATTLEE AND THE BRITISH LABOUR PARTY

At the end of World War II the British people were eager for a change. The Conservative Party had been in power since 1931. During his years as prime minister, Sir Winston Churchill (1874–1965) had led Britain to victory, but Britain no longer felt the need for war leadership.

The Conservative Party's prewar record did not match its war-time success. The Conservatives were slow to enact measures to overcome the miseries of the Great Depression. Chamberlain's appeasement policy was not only a failure but also a disgrace. The Conservative Party's further failure to begin rearmament left Britain scrambling to catch up in the face of Nazi aggression.

The Labour Party, by contrast, had no embarrassing prewar record to overcome. Moreover, Labour was a highly visible and effective coalition partner in Churchill's wartime government. In fact, Labour MP (member of Parliament) Clement Attlee served as Churchill's deputy prime minister.

Clement Attlee

Clement Attlee (1883–1967) was an unlikely labor leader. He was small, painfully shy, and handicapped by family money. After three years at Oxford he became a lawyer but took very few cases. Instead, he lived on an annual allowance from his father and spent what he later described as "a good deal of time practicing billiards."

In 1905 his brother Laurence convinced him to visit a boys' club in the Limehouse district of East London. He soon became a regular volunteer. In 1906 he became the club's resident manager.

Attlee had found his purpose in life. The poverty that he saw every day outraged him. The "abundant instances of kindness and much quiet heroism in these mean streets" inspired him to embrace socialism.

His first stop was the Fabian Society, where he was intimidated and uncomfortable. He found his home in Keir Hardie's Independent Labour Party, where he worked his way up through the ranks, doing the odd jobs that no one else had the time or inclination to do.

Churchill and Attlee on the Campaign Trail

When the election was announced in 1944, Attlee and Churchill hit the campaign trail. Churchill traveled in a motorcade. Attlee traveled in his own car, driven erratically by his wife. Churchill preached on the dangers of socialism. Attlee's mild-mannered presence refuted Churchill's rhetoric.

Attlee's platform was simple:

If in war, in spite of the diversion of energies to the making instruments of destruction and in spite of the shortage of supply, it was possible to provide food, clothing, and employment for all the people, it was not impossible to do the same in peace, provided the Government had the will and the power to act.

There was little doubt in the minds of the British public that they could expect more social reform from Labor than from the Conservatives. In July 1945, a month before Japan's surrender, the British electorate celebrated the end of the war by voting out Winston Churchill's war government.

The Labour Party was elected with a mandate for change. With a majority of 146 seats in the House of Commons, Clement Attlee formed a Labour government that became known for the scope of its reforms.

The Beveridge Report

In 1941 Winston Churchill commissioned William Beveridge (1879–1963) to create a report on how Britain should be rebuilt after the war. The resulting *Social Insurance and Allied Services* (1942), also known as The Beveridge Report, was adopted by Clement Attlee's Labour government as a blueprint for Britain's post–World War II welfare state.

A protégée of Beatrice Webb, Beveridge was an obvious choice to write the report. His lifelong interest in solutions for unemployment began in 1908 when he served as the sub-warden of a London settlement house. His first book, *Unemployment: A Problem of Industry* (1909), led to him being asked to advise Asquith's Liberal government on the formation of their national insurance and pension legislation.

The Settlement Movement

The settlement movement, popular from the 1880s to the 1920s, held that poverty could be alleviated if the rich and poor lived together in interdependent communities. The movement built settlement houses in poor urban areas, where middle-class, volunteer "settlement workers" lived and provided education and services to their neighbors. The best-known settlement house in America was Chicago's Hull House.

In *Social Insurance and Allied Services* Beveridge laid out three guiding principles for the government to follow in combating what he called the "five giants on the road of reconstruction": want, disease, ignorance, squalor, and idleness.

"Sectional interests" formed in the past should not limit proposals for the future: "A revolutionary moment in the world's history is a time for revolutions, not for patching."

Social insurance should be only part of a "comprehensive package of social progress."

Policies of social security should be achieved through cooperation between the state and the individual. The state "should not stifle incentive, opportunity, responsibility; in establishing a national minimum, it should leave room and encouragement for voluntary action by each individual to provide more than that minimum for himself and his family."

The proposals that followed included a free National Health Service that would prevent medical bills from becoming a source of poverty and a commitment to full employment to ensure that wages were there to help fund benefits.

Beveridge opposed means-tested benefits, arguing that they created a poverty trap for their recipients, making them unable to afford to make small improvements to their situations for fear of losing their safety nets. Instead, he proposed a flat-rate contribution from everyone and a flat-rate benefit for everyone. This principle of universality became one of the defining characteristics of welfare socialism.

The Beveridge Report was an unexpected bestseller. Eager to get a copy, people lined up outside the Stationery Office the night before it was released, as excited as if it were the latest volume in the Harry Potter series. More than 100,000 copies were sold the first month; 800,000 copies were sold in total. It was translated into twenty-two languages, distributed to the British troops, and airdropped over Nazi Germany. Beveridge became an unlikely popular hero, known as "The People's William."

THE BRITISH WELFARE STATE

Between 1945 and 1951 Attlee's government built the British welfare system using The Beveridge Report as its guide. The National Insurance Act provided retirement pensions, unemployment benefits, sick pay, maternity benefits, and funeral benefits. The Industrial Injuries Act paid for occupational disabilities. The National Health Service Act, passed in spite of the hostility of Britain's medical community, made complete medical care available to all residents of Britain.

Nationalization

During the same period, the Labor government nationalized the Bank of England, railways, long-distance hauling, telecommunications, coal mines, civil aviation, canals and docks, electricity, gas, and the iron and steel industries. All were basic to the economy or public utilities. None of them was flourishing prior to nationalization, with the exception of long-distance hauling.

The idea of introducing industrial democracy or worker control over the nationalized industries was never considered. Government-appointed boards managed the nationalized industries. Unlike the seizure of major industries in Russia, former owners were compensated for their property.

The only serious opposition to Attlee's program of nationalization came over the iron and steel industries, which were stable and had good relationships with their unions. The act of nationalizing these industries was the only measure proposed during Labour's term in office that the House of Lords delayed. The act became law in 1949, and took effect in 1951.

Soon after the law took effect, Labour lost the general election. The Conservative Party reprivatized iron and steel as soon as they took office in 1951. Iron and steel were the only industries to be returned to the private sector prior to the 1980s.

THE SCANDINAVIAN MODEL

Socialism in the North

The Swedish Social Democratic Labor Party (SAP) pioneered the creation of "mixed economies," which combined largely private ownership of the means of production with government direction of the economy and substantial welfare programs. Other nations' socialist parties followed their lead.

HJALMAR BRANTING

Hjalmar Branting (1860–1925) was the driving force behind the formation of the Swedish Social Democratic Labor Party in 1889. The son of one of the developers of the Swedish school of gymnastics, Branting was educated in the exclusive Beskow School in Stockholm and studied mathematics at the University of Uppsala. After graduating, he took a position as the assistant to the director of the Stockholm Observatory in 1882.

Traveling across Europe the following year, he stumbled across socialist doctrines everywhere. He attended lectures in Paris by revolutionary Marxist Paul Lafargue. He learned about social democracy from Eduard Bernstein in Zurich. He discussed revolution in Russia.

In 1889 Branting and trade union leader August Palm (1849–1922) formed the Swedish Social Democratic Labor Party, taking the German Social Democratic Party as their model. At its initial congress the party passed a resolution disclaiming any intention of violent revolution.

Branting was elected to the Lower Chamber of the Riksdag (parliament) in 1896. He remained the only socialist in the parliament until 1902, when the social democrats won four of the 230 seats in the Lower Chamber. At the next election they won thirteen. By 1917 the social democrats controlled enough seats to unbalance the two-party system. They formed a short-lived coalition government with the Liberals, with Branting as minister of finance.

THE GREAT DEPRESSION AND SWEDEN'S FIRST SOCIAL DEMOCRATIC GOVERNMENT

The full impact of the Great Depression reached Sweden in March 1932, when the collapse of "match king" Ivar Kreuger's business empire nearly brought down the Swedish banking system. During World War I Kreuger succeeded in bringing Sweden's match production into a single firm. After the war he tried to expand his monopoly worldwide, often using short-term credit from Swedish banks to make long-term loans to countries that were short of foreign currency in exchange for agreements giving him a monopoly. By 1928 Kreuger controlled more than half of the match production in the world. With the onset of the global depression, Kreuger's ability to juggle his debt burden failed. He killed himself on March 12, 1932.

A number of Swedish banks that had loaned Kreuger money had to be bailed out by the Swedish government. Kreuger's failure affected more than the banking system. He had extensive holdings in other Swedish companies. When his shares were dumped on the market, stock prices spiraled down. Personal fortunes evaporated and export sales fell. Production dropped 34 percent in the export industries and 13 percent in domestic industries. The number of unemployed workers rose from a pre-depression low of 10,000 to 189,225 in 1933.

Wigforss and Hansson Tame Unemployment

In 1931, months before the collapse of Kreuger's matchstick empire, economist Ernst Wigforss (1881–1977) developed a radical program of massive government intervention to fight unemployment and stimulate economic recovery. His program rested on two basic ideas:

1. The systematic use of government-financed public works to provide employment and stimulate the economy.
2. An effort to increase purchasing power using deficit government financing and redistribution of income in the form of social services and subsidies to the industrial working classes and farmers.

The Swedish Social Democratic Labor Party (SAP) took Wigforss's program to the polls in the 1932 elections, winning more than 40 percent of the vote.

Under the leadership of Per Albin Hansson (1885–1946), who served as premier four times between 1932 and 1946, the SAP implemented a reform plan based on Wigforss's program. With the informal support of the Agrarian Party, the SAP government transformed an existing system of relief work into a dynamic public works program. They began work immediately on any state and municipal public works that were already on the planning board for the future: schools, hospitals, railways, roads, harbor construction, and improvements in forestry and agriculture. The old relief system paid workers 15 percent less than the minimum wage an unskilled worker could earn in the open market. Men employed on the new public works program were paid a full market wage. The government borrowed money to fund the public works projects rather than raising the money through taxes, which would have neutralized the stimulus to the economy.

Social Democratic Rule

Between 1932 and 1976 the Swedish Social Democratic Labor Party ruled Sweden without interruption. Since 1976 the SAP has been removed from office four times: in 1976, 1991, 2006, and 2010. The first three changes in government brought no major shifts in Sweden's social welfare programs.

At the same time, the government introduced new social security measures, which were designed both to provide an economic safety net for the poor and to increase their purchasing power: unemployment insurance, increased old-age pensions, and housing loans for large families. They also implemented guaranteed prices for agricultural goods, special grants for rebuilding farm buildings, and easier access to agricultural credit. (The same banks that were willing to lend Ivar Kreuger millions were less welcoming to small farmers.) Sweden paid for these services through a progressive income tax. Altogether the Wigforss program reduced unemployment from 189,225 in 1933 to 9,600 in 1937.

FOLKHEMMET

The key idea in Swedish social democracy is *folkhemmet*: the concept that the society and state are the people's home. Per Albin Hansson described the concept of *folkhemmet* in an often-quoted statement:

> The basis of the home is togetherness and common feeling. The good home does not consider anyone either as privileged or unappreciated; it knows no special favourites and no stepchildren. There no one looks down upon anyone else, there no one tries to gain advantage at another's expense, and the stronger do not suppress and plunder the weaker. In the good home, equality, consideration, co-operation, and helpfulness prevail. Applied to the great people's and citizen's home this would mean the breaking down of all the social and economic barriers that now divide citizens into the privileged and the unfortunate, into rulers and subjects.

THATCHER AND PRIVATIZATION IN THE UK

The Clock Turns Back

Margaret Thatcher (1925–2013), born Margaret Roberts, became Britain's first female prime minister on May 3, 1979. Unlike many leaders of the Conservative Party, who have typically come from privileged backgrounds, Thatcher grew up in a cold-water flat above her parents' grocery store. During her childhood her father held a number of local political offices, including justice of the peace, town alderman, and mayor.

Thatcher was interested in politics from an early age. While studying chemistry at Oxford, she became one of the few woman presidents of the Oxford University Conservative Association. After she graduated in 1946, she worked as a research chemist for four years, reading for the bar in her spare time. In 1954 she began working as a barrister, specializing in tax law. Like many self-made successes, Thatcher believed in the power of individual enterprise and rejected the value of state support.

Thatcher As Education Minister

Thatcher's record as education minister illustrates her underlying political philosophy. During her tenure Thatcher eliminated a program providing free milk to schoolchildren, causing opponents to call her "Thatcher the milk snatcher." On the other hand, she also created more comprehensive schools than any prior education minister, providing a rigorous academic education to working-class children.

Thatcher first ran for Parliament in 1950, while still in her twenties. She lost but increased the Conservative vote for the district by 50 percent. In 1959 she was elected as the member of Parliament for the "safe" conservative district of Finchley. When she took her seat, she was the youngest woman in the House of Commons. She rose quickly within the Conservative Party. By 1970 she was a member of Edward Heath's Conservative government, holding the position of secretary of state for education and science.

After Heath lost two successive elections in 1974, Thatcher challenged him for the Conservative Party's leadership. With the backing of the party's right wing, she was elected party leader in 1975. In 1976 a speech against communism won her the sobriquet "the Iron Lady" in the Soviet press, a tag she carried with apparent pride.

BRITAIN'S "WINTER OF DISCONTENT"

Thatcher led the Conservative Party to a decisive victory in 1979, following what the press dubbed Britain's "winter of discontent." In the winter of 1978–1979 inflation was hovering at 25 percent. Prime Minister James Callaghan's Labour government sought to control the rate of inflation by capping pay increases at 5 percent. Unions responded with widespread strikes that resulted in gas and food shortages, power cuts, uncollected garbage, and hospital care limited to emergency cases. An unofficial strike by gravediggers in Liverpool provided images of unburied coffins that inflamed an already exasperated public.

THATCHERISM

During her first term as prime minister, from 1979 to 1983, Thatcher began by fulfilling her campaign promise to cut the power of the unions. Supported by memories of six weeks of rotting garbage and unburied coffins, the Conservative government passed a series of measures designed to limit the unions' power to strike, including laws that banned closed union shops, required unions to poll their members before organizing strikes, and made sympathy strikes illegal.

Mineworkers' Strike

The National Union of Mineworkers' 1984 strike was emblematic of Thatcher's relationship with the unions. The mineworkers went on strike to prevent the government from closing twenty coal mines that were deemed unproductive. The strike lasted nearly a year. Thatcher refused to meet the union's demands. In the end the miners returned to work without winning a single concession.

Having pulled the unions' fangs, Thatcher struck out at what she dismissed as the "nanny state." She introduced budget cuts for social services, such as education, the National Health Service, the social security system, and public housing. At the same time, she reduced or eliminated governmental regulations and subsidies to businesses and privatized state-owned industries and services. She also attacked inflation by limiting the amount of money printed, following Milton Friedman's theory of monetarism.

Thatcher successfully reduced inflation, but unemployment doubled between 1979 and 1981. She was elected to a second term by a landslide, owing in part to her decisive leadership in the Falkland

Islands War (1982) and to deep divisions in the Labour Party, which ran on a radical platform that critics called "the longest suicide note in history."

In her second term Thatcher began to sell shares in companies that were previously state-owned, tripling the number of individual stockholders in the country by the end of the 1980s. The government also sold 1.5 million publicly owned houses to their tenants. Both policies brought supporters to the Conservative Party. Meanwhile, the disparity in income between the wealthy and the working class increased.

In 1989 Thatcher pushed a flat-rate poll tax through Parliament, which led to violent riots. Spurred by public disapproval of the poll tax and Thatcher's increasingly strident tone, Conservative members of Parliament moved against her in November 1990. She defeated her senior opponent but did not have enough votes to retain the party leadership. Instead of contesting the election with a second ballot, Thatcher resigned from office as Conservative Party leader and prime minister on November 22, 1990, leaving behind crippling unemployment and rising welfare costs.

Monetarism

The economic theory of monetarism holds that the rate at which an economy grows is linked to increases in the economy's money supply. Monetarists believe that the government can promote economic stability by controlling the rate of growth of the money supply.

SOCIALISM IN THE DEVELOPING WORLD

From Kibbutzes to Nasser

Socialism in developing nations has been tightly interwoven with nationalism. As European colonies in Asia, Africa, and the Middle East won their independence in the years after World War II, many of them created socialist governments. Some combined aspects of indigenous traditions with the Marxist-Leninist model of one-party rule. Others followed the gradualist policies of the social democrats or the Fabian Society. Most received aid from the Soviet Union and/or the People's Republic of China, which saw the newly formed socialist regimes as chess pieces in the Cold War.

THE KIBBUTZ MOVEMENT IN ISRAEL

The kibbutz movement was an outgrowth of Zionism. Although Jews had long dreamed of returning to Israel, the political movement known as Zionism took shape at the end of the nineteenth century in Central and Eastern Europe. Zionism was nationalism with a twist: Instead of reclaiming their nation from a colonial power, members of the Jewish diaspora wanted to build a homeland for their nation.

Emigration to Palestine

The Zionist movement accelerated after the failed Russian Revolution of 1905. A wave of pogroms inspired an increase in emigration among Russian Jews. Many went to America. Others decided to try the Zionist dream and go to Palestine as pioneer settlers.

The first kibbutz was founded at Degania in 1909 on land owned by the Jewish National Fund. Others were created in the following years. By 1914 there were roughly 90,000 Jews in Palestine, 13,000 of them living in agricultural settlements. By the early twenty-first century there were more than 250 kibbutzim in Israel, with a total population of more than 100,000.

What Is a Kibbutz?

There are two different types of cooperative settlements in Israel: the moshav and the kibbutz. In a moshav each family is an economic and social unit that lives in its own house and works its own fields. Although each farm family is independent, the village cooperative purchases supplies and markets produce. The cooperative also provides the farmer with credit and other services. The first settlements of this type were founded in Jezreel Valley in 1921.

A kibbutz is a true collective that holds all wealth in common and pools both labor and income. Most kibbutzim are agricultural, but a few have expanded into industrial production. Most members work on the kibbutz itself. Kibbutz members receive no salary or wages because the kibbutz fulfills all the members' needs.

At first the kibbutz community took precedence over the family. Adults had private quarters, and children were housed and cared for as a group. Today, most children sleep in their parents' house but spend their days with their peer group. Cooking and dining are communal. Profits are reinvested in the settlement after members have been provided with food, clothing, shelter, and social and medical services.

NEHRU'S INDIA

Before he met Mohandas Gandhi, Jawaharlal Nehru (1889–1964) was an Englishman in Indian clothing. After studying at home under a series of English governesses and tutors, he was sent to school in England at the age of fifteen. Known to his English friends as "Joe Nehru," he attended Harrow and Cambridge, where he earned a degree in natural sciences, with a minor in actresses and social life, and then read for the bar at the Inns of Court in London. He spent his vacations traveling in Europe. In 1912 Nehru returned to India, with little enthusiasm, to practice law with his father, the prominent barrister Motilal Nehru.

Motilal Nehru was already active in the Indian nationalist movement and a leader in the Indian National Congress, which at the time was fighting for dominion status within the British Empire. Jawaharlal Nehru joined his father as a Congress member in 1918, with the same lack of enthusiasm that he brought to the practice of law.

Involvement in the Independence Movement

In 1919 Jawaharlal Nehru overheard General R.H. Dyer boasting about the recent massacre of Indian protesters at Jallianwala Bagh, in which Dyer ordered Gurkha soldiers to fire on thousands of Indians gathered for a religious observance in a public park. Outraged, Nehru became seriously involved in the independence movement: touring rural India, organizing nationalist volunteers, and making public speeches. Under Gandhi's influence, Nehru abandoned his Westernized lifestyle and began wearing clothes made from *khadi* (homespun cotton cloth), studying the *Bhagavad Gita*, and practicing yoga.

When India achieved independence from Great Britain in 1947, Nehru became the first prime minister and minister for external affairs, a dual position he held until his death in 1964.

Nehru believed that the answers to India's problems lay in socialist economic theory, but he didn't let his socialist convictions affect his foreign policy decisions. Instead of picking sides in the Cold War, he chose "positive neutrality" and served as a key spokesperson for the unaligned countries of Asia and Africa. On the domestic front he committed India to a policy of industrialization, reorganization of its states on a linguistic basis, and the development of a casteless, secular state.

Indira Gandhi

Nehru's daughter, Indira, became prime minister two years after her father's death, using her married name, Gandhi. (Her husband was no relation to Mohandas.) Between them, Indira and her son, Rajiv, held the position of prime minister for twenty years between 1966 and 1989.

Nehru and Gandhi agreed that poverty was India's greatest challenge after independence, but they disagreed on the solution. Gandhi, like many of the utopian socialists of the nineteenth century, believed the solution was self-sufficiency at the level of the village commune: shared labor and wealth, and a spinning wheel in every hut. Nehru looked for national self-sufficiency, based on "tractors and big machinery."

Under Nehru's leadership, India adopted a mixture of Fabian-style central planning and free enterprise to rebuild the country's ravaged economy. The government instituted a series of five-year plans intended to build India's production capabilities and improve agricultural yields. It also launched several major campaigns against rural poverty.

NASSER'S EGYPT

The son of a village post office clerk, Gamal Abdel Nasser (1918–1970) led his first demonstrations protesting British influence over Egypt's government and economy when he was sixteen. After graduating from secondary school, Nasser spent several months as a law student before he gave in and took the easiest path to upward mobility—the army. He entered the Egyptian Royal Military Academy in 1936, graduating as a second lieutenant.

Revolution and Reform

On July 23, 1952, following a breakdown of law and order in Cairo, Nasser and eighty-nine other Free Officers carried out a bloodless coup against King Farouk, who spent the rest of his life in exile in Monaco. A year later Nasser emerged as the unquestioned leader of Egypt.

With his new government in place, Nasser began a program of reforms based on what he described as "Arab socialism," which was derived from a rejection of imperialism rather than class struggle. He believed that state ownership or control of the means of production and redistribution of income were necessary to make Egypt strong.

Criticism of Arab Socialism

Nasser's "Arab socialism" drew complaints from devout Muslims and Marxists alike. The extremist Muslim Brotherhood accused Nasser of camouflaging a secular policy with Islamic language. Marxists claimed that since "Arab socialism" wasn't based on the concept of class struggle, it wasn't socialism at all.

Agrarian Reforms

Nasser's first major reforms were agrarian. Beginning with King Farouk's extensive personal holdings, large estates were broken up and distributed to peasant families. The law in 1953 limited land ownership to 200 feddans per family. Subsequent legislation further limited ownership to 100 and later 50 feddans. Along with land redistribution, Nasser's government introduced state-controlled agricultural cooperatives to provide farmers with credit, fertilizer, and seeds, began a program to reclaim land from the desert, and extended labor laws to cover agricultural workers.

The controversial nationalization of the Suez Canal in 1956 was only the first step in a program designed to bring the economy under centralized government control. In 1960 and 1961 banks and major industries were nationalized, and direct government control was imposed on important sectors of the economy, including insurance and transportation. Only retail businesses and housing were left in private hands.

The creation of a centralized economy was accompanied by the implementation of social reforms. Nasser's government introduced new protections for labor, and extended public health services and a system of industrial profit sharing that funded insurance and welfare services.

The National Charter

In 1962 Nasser submitted a document called *The National Charter* to the National Congress of the short-lived United Arab Republic. In ten short chapters he outlined the ideological foundation of Arab socialism. The charter begins with a list of the six principles that led to the 1952 revolution:

1. To end imperialism
2. To end the system of feudal landlords

3. To end the domination of capital over the government
4. To establish a basis of social justice
5. To build a powerful national army
6. To establish a sound democratic system

It ends with a call for Arab unity.

THE COLLAPSE OF THE SOVIET UNION

Glasnost and *Perestroika*

In early August 1980 workers across Poland went on strike to protest rising food prices. In Gdańsk some 17,000 workers at the Lenin Shipyard staged a strike and barricaded themselves inside. By mid-August the strike was losing steam. Shipyard director Klemens Gniech assured strikers that he would negotiate for their demands if they went back to work. It was tempting, even though Gniech had not kept his promises in the past.

The strike gained new life when electrician Lech Wałęsa climbed over the shipyard wall, jumped onto a bulldozer, and urged the striking workers on. The reinvigorated strikers elected Wałęsa as the head of a strike committee to negotiate with management.

Lech Wałęsa

Lech Wałęsa (1943–) began work at the Lenin Shipyard as an electrician in 1967. He emerged as a union activist during anti-government protests in 1976, and consequently lost his job. For the next four years he earned a living doing temporary jobs and worked with other activists to organize free, noncommunist trade unions.

Three days later the strikers' demands were met. When other strikers in the city asked Wałęsa to continue his strike out of solidarity, he agreed. Wałęsa established the Interfactory Strike Committee, which united industrial workers in the Gdańsk area into a single bargaining unit. Within a week the committee had presented the Polish government with a list of demands that included the right to strike and form free unions and declared a general strike. On August 31 the Gdańsk strikers and the Polish government signed an agreement that granted free and independent unions the right to strike, and also provided greater freedom of religions and political expression.

THE INDEPENDENT SELF-GOVERNING TRADE UNION SOLIDARITY

Throughout 1981 the communist government of Wojciech Jaruzelski was faced with a series of controlled strikes by the independent trade union Solidarity, in conjunction with demands for economic reforms, free elections, and the involvement of trade unions at the highest level of decision-making. Both Wałęsa and Jaruzelski were pressured into extreme positions: Wałęsa by more militant unionists, and Jaruzelski by the Soviet Union. On December 13 Jaruzelski declared martial law. Solidarity was declared illegal and its leaders, included Wałęsa, were arrested. On October 8, 1982, the Polish parliament officially dissolved the union. Solidarity continued to operate underground.

Nobel Prize

Lech Wałęsa received the Nobel Peace Prize in 1983. Still operating underground, Solidarity members were heartened by the award. The Polish government was less enthusiastic. Fearing that Wałęsa would not be able to return to Poland if he left, his wife traveled to Stockholm to accept the prize on his behalf.

In 1988 collapsing economic conditions set off a new wave of labor unrest in Poland. With no support from the USSR, demands that the government recognize Solidarity forced Jaruzelski to negotiate. In April 1989 the Polish government agreed to legalize Solidarity and allow it to participate in elections. In the free elections held that June, Solidarity candidates won ninety-nine out of one hundred seats in the newly formed Polish Senate, and all of the 161 seats that opposition candidates were allowed to contest in the lower house. In August longtime Solidarity supporter Tadeusz Mazowiecki became the first noncommunist head of government in the Eastern Bloc.

MIKHAIL GORBACHEV OPENS THE DOOR

Born into a peasant family in the Stavropol territory of Russia, Mikhail Gorbachev (1931–) joined the Young Communist League as soon as he was old enough to become a member. He spent several years driving a combine on a state farm before he enrolled in law school at Moscow University and became a member of the Communist Party. After he graduated in 1955, Gorbachev gained the attention of high-ranking Soviet officials, in part because of his work as the head of the Stavropol region's agricultural department and in part because several popular hot water spas were located in the region. In 1971 he was elected to the Communist Party's Central Committee. He became a full member of the Politburo in 1980.

As a forty-nine-year-old among the eighty-somethings in the Politburo, Gorbachev became one of its most active and visible members. In the mid-1980s three general secretaries of the Communist

Party of the Soviet Union (CPSU) died in quick succession. Following Leonid Brezhnev (1906–1982), who served as general secretary from 1977 to 1982, Yuri Andropov (1914–1984) held the office for fifteen months. His successor, Konstantin Chernenko (1911–1985), died after only eleven months. On March 11, 1985, the Politburo elected its youngest member, Mikhail Gorbachev, to the post.

Gorbachev's primary goal was to rescue the stagnant Soviet economy. At first he tried the timeworn Soviet method of calling for rapid modernization of technology and greater worker productivity. It was not enough. As Gorbachev described the problem, "The very system was dying away; its sluggish senile blood no longer contained any vital juices."

USSR, Not Russia

The USSR was often referred to as Russia. In fact, the Union of Soviet Socialist Republics, informally known as the Soviet Union, was a federation of fifteen Soviet republics that were created out of the remains of the Russian empire in 1917. Russia was the dominant republic within the federation.

In 1986 Gorbachev decided to try something new. He introduced two major economic and political policies: *glasnost* (openness) and *perestroika* (restructuring).

Implementing the new policy of *glasnost*, Gorbachev relaxed previous restrictions on freedom of speech and the press. He released thousands of political prisoners, including dissident physicist Andrei Sakharov.

Under the new policy of *perestroika*, Gorbachev took steps to untangle the government's legislative and executive branches from the CPSU. "We need democracy like air," he announced. In December

SOCIALISM 101

1988 a new bicameral parliament called the USSR Congress of People's Deputies was elected in a contested election, with multiple candidates and secret ballots. Dissidents of all kinds replaced long-standing party officials, including Sakharov, who was elected as the representative of the Soviet Academy of Sciences. In 1989 the new Congress elected a new Supreme Soviet from its ranks, with Gorbachev as chairman. Similar legislatures were established in each of the Soviet republics.

In March 1990 Gorbachev took further steps to transfer political power from the CPSU to elected government institutions. Under pressure from him, the Congress of People's Deputies elected him to the newly created post of the president of the USSR and abolished the Communist Party's constitutional monopoly on political power in the Soviet Union.

THE COLLAPSE OF SOVIET COMMUNISM

At the same time that Gorbachev was introducing political reforms into the USSR, he was encouraging reform in the Soviet-bloc countries of Eastern Europe.

In an ironic reversal of the domino theory (the idea that when one allied state collapses, others will follow), the communist states of Eastern and Central Europe fell one by one and were replaced by noncommunist states. In September 1989 Poland convened its first noncommunist government since 1948. A week later the communist regime in Hungary began talks with its opposition. Massive demonstrations on both sides of the Berlin Wall brought about the collapse of the East German government in October. By the end of 1990 there were noncommunist governments in power in Romania, Bulgaria, Czechoslovakia, Albania, and Hungary.

The decentralization of the USSR's political system and the example of new, noncommunist governments throughout Eastern Europe led to the rise of ethnic and nationalist independence movements in the member states of the Soviet Union. In 1991 Gorbachev proposed a referendum on whether to hold the Soviet Union together. Six of the fifteen republics refused to participate. The Russian Republic agreed to participate but added a second question to the referendum, asking whether Russia should establish its own presidency. Russian voters said "yes" to both proposals. Three months later Boris Yeltsin was elected president of the Russian Federation, and a treaty for a new union between the republics was under negotiation.

Faced with the end of the USSR, Communist Party hardliners rebelled. In August 1991 a group of senior CPSU officials broke into Gorbachev's vacation home and placed him under house arrest. They demanded that he declare a state of emergency. When he refused, they issued a decree in the name of the State Committee on the State of Emergency. The days of compliant obedience to party decrees were over. Hundreds of thousands of citizens poured into the streets to defend the government, led by Yeltsin, who stood on top of a tank and denounced the "right-wing, reactionary, anti-constitutional *coup d'état.*" Faced with resistance, not to mention the shock of being called "right-wing" after a lifetime in the Communist Party, the coup leaders retreated.

Gorbachev resigned as the first and only president of the USSR on December 25, 1991. On December 26 the Supreme Soviet, which had ruled the USSR since 1917, dissolved itself.

SOCIALIST MOVEMENTS IN THE US

From De Leon to Debs

Daniel De Leon (1852–1914) was born in Curaçao in the Dutch Antilles. After being educated in England and Germany, he came to America in 1874. While a student and later a teacher at Columbia University, he was converted to socialism through the writings of Edward Bellamy.

In 1890 De Leon joined the Socialist Labor Party, which had replaced the First International in 1877. He wrote the party's first formal platform, calling for the replacement of the capitalist state with a workers' democracy and a socialist reorganization of the economy. In 1891 he ran as the Socialist Labor Party's candidate for governor of New York, winning only 13,000 votes.

De Leon was one of the chief propagandists for socialism in the American labor movement. He argued for the revolutionary over-throw of capitalism in the United States, claiming that since America was the most developed country, it was "ripe for the execution of Marxian revolutionary tactics." The only thing missing was a fully developed proletariat class consciousness.

Since American society was ready for revolution, De Leon believed, reform was not only unnecessary; it was counterproductive. Instead, the socialist party should concentrate on transforming American labor into a class capable of its own liberation by providing them with "the proper knowledge." Since forming trade unions was an instinctive act on the part of the worker, a result of the small amount of class consciousness already present in the proletariat, the natural vehicle for working-class education was the trade unions. Once the socialists won control of the state, the party would dissolve, leaving the administration of production in the hands of the industrial unions.

In 1895 De Leon founded the Socialist Trade and Labor Alliance. The organization's founding documents declared that the "methods and spirit of labor organization are absolutely impotent to resist the aggressions of concentrated capital." American labor apparently disagreed. De Leon's Alliance had only 13,000 members at its height compared to more than one million members in the American Federation of Labor (AFL) at the same time.

EUGENE V. DEBS: SOCIALIST FOR PRESIDENT

Born in Terre Haute, Indiana, labor organizer Eugene V. Debs (1855–1926) left home when he was fourteen to work for the railroad. In 1875 he helped organize a local lodge of the Brotherhood of Locomotive Firemen. He rose rapidly in the organization, becoming its national secretary and treasurer in 1880. In 1893 he became president of the newly established American Railway Union, which successfully united railway workers from different crafts into the first industrial union in the United States.

Debs was dubbed "King Debs" in the national press after his union successfully struck for higher wages from the Great Northern Railway in April 1894.

The Pullman Strike

During the economic depression known as the Panic of 1893, the Pullman Palace Car Company cut its wages by 25 percent. It did not cut rents for workers' housing in Pullman, Illinois, its company town near Chicago. Local members of the American Railway Union sent a delegation to talk to Pullman's president, George M. Pullman. He refused to meet with them. In response, the union's national council called for a nationwide boycott of trains carrying Pullman cars. Within four days union locals in twenty-seven states had gone out on sympathy strikes, affecting twenty-nine railroads.

Illinois governor John P. Altgeld sympathized with the strikers and refused to call out the militia, so the railroads' management called on the federal government for help. On July 2 US Attorney General Richard Olney got an injunction against the strike from local judges on the grounds that the union was impeding mail service and interstate commerce. Union leaders ignored the injunction. On July 4 President Grover Cleveland ordered 2,500 federal troops to Chicago. The strike ended within a week, and troops were recalled on July 20. Debs was sentenced to six months in jail for contempt of court and conspiring against interstate commerce.

Debs Converts to Socialism

During his prison term in Woodstock, Illinois, Debs read broadly. Introduced for the first time to the work of Karl Marx, he came to see the labor movement as a struggle between classes.

After announcing his conversion to socialism in 1897, Debs joined forces with journalist Victor Berger to found the Social Democratic Party, renamed the Socialist Party in 1901. Debs ran as the Socialist Party candidate for president five times between 1900 and 1920. His highest popular vote came in 1920, when he received about 915,000 votes. Debs was in prison at the time, serving a sentence for criticizing the federal government's use of the 1917 Espionage Act and 1918 Sabotage Act.

FROM THE IWW TO THE PALMER RAIDS

Socialism Grows in America

The Industrial Workers of the World (IWW), popularly known as "the Wobblies," was founded in 1905 by representatives of forty-three different labor groups who were opposed to the "pure and simple" unionism of Samuel Gompers's American Federation of Labor. The most extreme of America's pre–World War I labor groups, the IWW rejected political action, arbitration, and binding contracts. Instead, they put their faith in the strike and nothing but the strike. Inspired by European syndicalism, the IWW wanted to organize all workers into "One Big Union," with the ultimate goal of a revolutionary general strike that would overthrow capitalism and create a workers' society.

The principal founders of the IWW were Daniel De Leon of the Socialist Labor Party, Eugene V. Debs of the Socialist Party, and William D. ("Big Bill") Haywood of the Western Federation of Miners. De Leon and Debs came out of the social democratic tradition of the socialist left. Haywood's ideological base was the militant unionism of the Western Federation of Miners, which spent a decade fighting mine owners and the government in its efforts to unionize hard-rock miners and smelter workers.

In 1908 the Wobblies split into two factions. One faction, led by De Leon and Debs, argued for creating change through political action by socialist parties and labor unions. The other faction, led by Haywood, came down in favor of syndicalist-style direct action: general strikes, boycotts, and sabotage. The syndicalists won and expelled the socialists from the organization.

Under Haywood's leadership, the Wobblies adopted an American version of syndicalism: class warfare based on direct industrial action. The IWW's actions often led to arrests and sensational publicity. Haywood himself was arrested and acquitted on a labor-related murder charge in 1906–1907. The group led a number of important strikes in the East between 1907 and 1913, but its main area of operation was among western workers in mining, lumber, transportation, and agriculture.

"Organize As a Class"

"The working class and the employing class have nothing in common....Between these two classes a struggle must go on until the workers of the world organize as a class, take possession of the means of production, abolish the wage system, and live in harmony with the Earth." (Preamble, *IWW Constitution*)

The Effect of World War I on Socialism in America

The United States' entry into World War I in 1917 created a permanent break between socialists and the labor movement. When the war began, labor leaders and socialists alike called for neutrality. As soon as the United States entered the war, labor unions gave the government their wholehearted support. Socialists continued to oppose the war. Many were arrested under the 1917 Espionage Act and 1918 Sabotage Act, which made it illegal to undermine the war effort.

Opposition to the War

The IWW was the only labor organization to oppose US involvement in the war. They protested by attempting to limit copper production in the western states. The government responded by prosecuting IWW leaders under the newly enacted Espionage and Sabotage Acts.

The Bolshevik Revolution in October 1917 split the socialist party. Reform-minded moderates abhorred the Bolshevik takeover. More radical members applauded it. The moderates, who controlled the party, expelled those who supported the revolution. The radicals subsequently founded the American Communist Party.

THE FIRST RED SCARE

After the war Attorney General A. Mitchell Palmer became convinced that communists and socialists were planning to overthrow the government, in part because an Italian anarchist blew himself up outside Palmer's home in Washington. On the second anniversary of the Russian Revolution more than ten thousand suspected socialists, communists, and anarchists were arrested in what became known as the "Palmer Raids." Charged with advocating force, violence, and unlawful means to overthrow the government, the suspected revolutionaries were held without trial for an extended period. The courts ultimately found no evidence of a proposed revolution, and most were released. A small number, including Emma Goldman, were declared to be subversive aliens and deported to the Soviet Union.

FROM DEPRESSION TO NEW DEAL

Socialism Amid Capitalism

In 1932 America was in the depths of the Great Depression. The newly elected president, Franklin D. Roosevelt, promised a "New Deal" for everyone. In his first one hundred days in office Roosevelt pushed through fifteen major pieces of legislation, including programs designed to get Americans working again. These programs took three basic forms:

1. Short-term relief programs designed to alleviate suffering.
2. Long-term programs designed to help the economy recover.
3. Permanent reform programs designed to prevent, or reduce the impact of, future depressions.

Many of the programs instituted between 1933 and 1935 aimed at restoring the economy from the top down. The Agricultural Adjustment Act sought to stimulate farm prices by paying farmers to produce less. The National Industrial Recovery Act stabilized both prices and wages. Both programs failed to address the basic problem of weak consumer demand as a result of falling wages and rising unemployment.

Beginning in 1935 Roosevelt's reforms moved further left, driven in part by pressure from the socialist and populist left. Socialist Party presidential candidate Norman Thomas won three times as many votes in the 1932 election as he had in 1929. More than five million elderly Americans joined Townsend Clubs, supporting Dr. Francis Townsend's proposal of a federally funded old-age pension as a way to solve the problem of weak consumer demand. Louisiana senator Huey P. Long rose to national prominence with his "Share the Wealth" plan, which proposed a guaranteed household income for every American family, to be paid for by taxes on the wealthiest Americans. Father Charles E. Coughlin appealed to the urban poor with his call for nationalized industries and currency inflation.

Father Coughlin

Father Charles E. Coughlin (1891–1979) reached tens of millions of listeners with his weekly radio broadcasts. He supported Roosevelt against Herbert Hoover in the 1932 election. Over time he turned against the New Deal. His attacks against Communists, Jews, and Wall Street became increasingly shrill. In 1942 the Roman Catholic Church ordered Coughlin off the air.

New Deal programs introduced after 1935 were based on John Maynard Keynes's theory that depressions should be attacked by increasing the spending ability of the people at the bottom of the income pyramid.

The WPA Projects

The WPA hired 8.5 million men to build roads, public buildings, bridges, airports, and parks across America. The WPA also hired artists, writers, and actors for cultural programs that included creating art for public buildings, writing state guidebooks, collecting folklore in rural America, and organizing community theaters.

The Works Progress Administration (WPA) employed over eight million Americans between 1935 and 1943. The Social Security Act of 1935 set up a worker-funded, government-guaranteed pension system, similar to that called for by the Townsend Clubs. The National Labor

Relations Act, often called the Wagner Act after Senator Robert Wagner, guaranteed the right of collective bargaining for workers.

Assessments of Roosevelt's New Deal

Roosevelt's contemporaries at either end of the political spectrum condemned Roosevelt's policies. Right-wing groups denounced the New Deal as the first step toward a communist dictatorship. American communists branded the New Deal as a step toward fascism.

Scholarly assessments of the impact of the New Deal also break down along ideological lines:

- Conservative historians describe the Depression as an extreme market correction and the New Deal as the beginnings of a socialist welfare state, which they believe is an inherently bad thing, resulting in regulation and loss of freedom.
- Liberal historians describe the Depression as the failure of *laissez faire* economics and the New Deal as the beginnings of a democratic welfare state, which they believe is an inherently good thing, as government responds to the needs of the people.
- Leftist historians describe the Depression as the failure of capitalism and the New Deal as reformed capitalism.

The Impact of the New Deal on American Socialism

The Socialist Party lost much of its support when the New Deal came into effect. Roosevelt implemented many programs that were a part of the socialist program. More important, New Deal programs benefited the sections of society that had traditionally supported socialism. The "Roosevelt Coalition" of farmers, union members, working-class people, northern blacks, and liberals turned instead to the Democratic Party.

SENATOR JOSEPH MCCARTHY

The Second Red Scare

During the early 1950s communist advances into Eastern Europe and China frightened many Americans. Wisconsin Senator Joseph McCarthy (1908–1957) took those fears and turned them into an official witch hunt.

Born to a farm family near Appleton, Wisconsin, McCarthy left school at fourteen. He worked as a chicken farmer and managed a grocery store before he went back to high school at the age of twenty. He went on to earn a law degree from Marquette University.

The "Domino Theory"

During the Cold War, United States foreign policy was dominated by the "domino theory": the idea that if a noncommunist state "fell" to communism, it would lead to the fall of the noncommunist states around that country. The domino theory was first used by President Harry Truman to justify sending military aid to Greece and Turkey in the 1940s.

In 1948 Joseph McCarthy was elected to the United States Senate in an upset victory over incumbent Senator Robert La Follette Jr. McCarthy ran a dirty campaign. He lied about his war record, claiming to have flown thirty-two missions during World War II when he actually worked a desk job and flew only in training exercises. La Follette was too old for service when Pearl Harbor was bombed, but McCarthy attacked him for not enlisting and accused him of war profiteering.

On his first day as a senator McCarthy called a little-noticed press conference that was a tune-up for his later performance as a demagogue. He had a modest proposal for ending a coal strike that was in progress: Draft union leader John L. Lewis and the striking miners into the army. If they still continued to strike, they should be court-martialed for insubordination and then shot.

By 1950 McCarthy's senate career was in trouble. The story of how he lied about his war record during the election campaign became public. He was under investigation for tax offenses and for accepting bribes from the Pepsi-Cola Company to support removing wartime controls on sugar.

ATTACKS ON THE AMERICAN COMMUNIST PARTY

McCarthy deliberately directed attention away from his own failings. On February 9, 1950, speaking to a group of Republican women in Wheeling, West Virginia, McCarthy announced that he had a list of 205 State Department employees who were "card-carrying" members of the American Communist Party, some of whom were passing classified information to the Soviet Union. Suddenly McCarthy was in the headlines. When the Senate Committee on Foreign Relations asked McCarthy to testify, he was unable to provide the name of a single "card-carrying communist" in any government department.

Undeterred by the absence of facts, McCarthy began an anti-communist crusade in the national media. Playing on real popular fears, McCarthy used scare tactics to discredit his opponents. He began by claiming that communist subversives had infiltrated

President Truman's administration. When the Democrats accused McCarthy of smear tactics, he responded that their accusations were part of the communist conspiracy. As a result of his tactics, the Republicans swept the 1950 elections. The remaining Democrats in Congress were reluctant to criticize him. McCarthy, once voted "the worst U.S. senator" by the Senate press corps, was now one of the most influential men in the Senate.

McCarthyism

Following the 1952 election McCarthy became the chairman of the Committee on Government Operations of the Senate and of its permanent investigation subcommittee. In an ironic mirror image of Stalin's trials of alleged counterrevolutionaries, McCarthy held hearings against individuals he accused of being communists, and government agencies suspected of harboring them. He attacked journalists who criticized his hearings. He campaigned to have "anti-American" books removed from libraries. When Republican Dwight Eisenhower was elected in 1952, McCarthy attacked him for not being tough enough on communism.

McCarthy ran into trouble when he attempted to discredit the secretary of the Army. The Army leaked information to journalists who were known to oppose him. As a result, America saw McCarthy's bullying tactics firsthand in a televised thirty-six-day hearing in which the Army accused McCarthy of attempting to subvert military officers and civilian officials.

The Republicans lost control of the Senate in the midterm elections of 1954, in part because of the public's loss of confidence in McCarthy. With a vote of sixty-seven to twenty-two, the Senate subsequently censured McCarthy for conduct "contrary to senatorial traditions."

THE CUBAN REVOLUTION

Socialism on America's Doorstep

In 1895 Cuba rebelled against Spanish rule. Revolts and rebellions had been a way of life in Cuba for almost four hundred years, but this time things were different. Spanish efforts to repress the rebellion aroused popular sympathy in Cuba's big neighbor to the north. When the US battleship *Maine* mysteriously blew up in Havana's harbor on February 15, 1898, America declared war on Spain. Cuban hopes that American involvement meant independence were soon dashed. When the Spanish-American War ended, the United States continued to occupy Cuba. It began to look like Cuba had exchanged one colonial ruler for another.

When the Cuban Constitutional Convention met in July 1900, its members discovered that the United States intended to attach an amendment to their constitution. Written by American Secretary of State Elihu Root, the Platt Amendment allowed the United States to intervene in Cuban affairs whenever order was threatened, forbade the Cuban government to borrow money without American permission, and forced Cuba to lease land to the United States for naval bases. Cuba reluctantly accepted the Platt Amendment and became "independent" in May 1902.

For the next fifty years Cuban politics were shaped by economic dependence on sugar, frequent military coups, and regular interference in its internal affairs by the United States.

Beginning in 1933 successive Cuban governments depended on the support of military strongman Fulgencio Batista (1901–1973). In 1940 Batista was elected president in his own right. After completing a four-year term of office, he stepped down after he was defeated in a democratic election. In 1952 Batista ran for president again. Defeated for a second time, he overthrew the constitutional government and established a regime even more corrupt and repressive than those of his predecessors.

Platt Amendment Annulled

Franklin D. Roosevelt annulled the Platt Amendment in 1934 as part of his "Good Neighbor Policy" toward Latin America. Revoking the amendment made little practical difference. America still maintained a naval base at Guantanamo Bay. As Cuba's biggest trade partner, the United States continued to meddle in Cuban affairs.

FIDEL CASTRO

The son of a prosperous sugarcane farmer, Fidel Castro (1926–2016) was a committed political activist before he was twenty. While studying law at the University of Havana, Castro joined an unsuccessful attempt to overthrow General Rafael Trujillo in the Dominican Republic and took part in street riots in Colombia. After he received his degree in 1950, he seemed to settle down. He opened a law practice in Havana and became a member of a moderate reform party, the Cuban People's Party, also known as the *Ortodoxos*. He ran as that party's candidate for a seat in the House of Representatives in the 1952 elections.

Castro reverted to revolutionary tactics after Batista's 1952 coup. When legal means to overturn Batista failed, Castro attempted to start a revolution by attacking the Moncada military barracks with a group of 160 men on July 26, 1953. The attempt was a total failure.

Most of the attackers were killed. Castro and his brother Raúl were arrested and sentenced to fifteen years in prison. Released two years later as part of a general amnesty, the brothers went into self-imposed exile in Mexico, where they trained a small revolutionary force.

In late 1956 a small yacht landed Castro, Raúl, and a rebel force of eighty-one men on the southeastern coast of Cuba. The so-called 26th of July Movement was routed and almost destroyed by Batista's security forces. A dozen survivors retreated to the Sierra Maestra mountains and began a guerilla war against the Batista dictatorship. Over the next year they recruited more insurgents and built alliances with other revolutionary groups, including disaffected liberal politicians. By 1958 Batista's regime was in trouble. Several of his military leaders joined the revolutionaries. The United States government withdrew its support, hoping to reach an agreement with the revolutionary forces similar to the one it had with Batista and his predecessors. After all, political coups were nothing new in Cuba.

In December 1958 Batista fled the country, leaving Castro in power as the undisputed leader of the revolution.

Castro Rebuilds Cuba

Over the next few years Castro and the 26th of July Movement created the first socialist country in the Americas. Castro's initial program wasn't explicitly socialist. Its major features were land reforms and progressive tax policies aimed at foreign investors, the sugar industry, large businesses, and the tourist industries of Havana. Not surprisingly, he quickly gained a following of peasants, urban workers, and leftists of all varieties. The propertied classes were less enthusiastic. Many of them left Cuba for the United States.

Over the course of 1959 and 1960 Castro nationalized foreign businesses, established a centrally planned economy, and brought basic social services to poor and rural areas. In February 1960 he signed a trade deal with the Soviet Union. Already angry about the loss of nationalized property, the United States retaliated for Castro's new relationship with Russia by imposing a trade embargo, plotting to assassinate Castro, and supporting an unsuccessful invasion attempt by Cuban exiles at the Bay of Pigs. America's hard-line attitude only made Castro more popular in Cuba and forced him to become increasingly dependent on Soviet trade policies.

VIETNAM

The Radicalization of a Generation

The word *Vietnam* came to symbolize to a generation growing conflicts that divided the United States in the 1960s and 1970s. To some, it meant the United States carrying out its duty to protect smaller nations from threats by communists. To others, it meant a brutal war against a people struggling for freedom. In the leadership of Vietnam's quest for independence was a small, withered old man with an iron will: Ho Chi Minh.

HO CHI MINH AND THE STRUGGLE FOR INDEPENDENCE

Ho Chi Minh (1890–1969), born Nguyen Sinh Cung, grew up in the French possession of Indochina. Formed in 1887, French Indochina originally included Cambodia and the Vietnamese regions of Annam, Tonkin, and Cochinchina. Laos was added in 1893. Ho's father was a scholar who lost his position due to his political views. He scraped together a meager living writing and reading letters for illiterate peasants.

Ho received a French education and spent several years as a schoolteacher. In 1911, at the age of twenty-one, he decided to join the navy and see the world. He spent three years working as a cook on a French steamer. After living in London for several years, he moved to France, where he became an active socialist and anti-colonial activist. Working under the name Nguyen Ai Quoc (Nguyen the Patriot), he organized a group of expatriate Vietnamese and was one of the founders of the French Communist Party. In 1919 he addressed a petition to the Versailles Peace Conference calling on the French to give their Indochinese subjects equal rights. The members of the conference ignored him, but he caught the attention of politically conscious Vietnamese as someone to watch.

Ho left France in 1923. He spent the next ten years traveling between communist strongholds and organizing expatriate Vietnamese nationalists. In 1924 he played an active role in the Fifth Congress of the Communist International, taking the French Communist Party to task for not opposing colonialism more vigorously. Later that year he traveled to Canton, China, under the assumed name of Ly Thuy, where he organized Vietnamese nationalists who had been exiled from Indochina for their political beliefs into the Viet Nam Thanh Nien Cach Menh Dong Chi Hoi (Vietnam Revolutionary Youth Association), better known as the Thanh Nien. When Chiang Kai-shek expelled the communists from Canton in 1927, Ho went on the road again, traveling to Moscow, Brussels, and Paris before settling in Siam (now Thailand) as the Comintern's representative in Southeast Asia.

In 1930 Ho Chi Minh returned to Vietnam to preside over the formation of the Indochinese Communist Party (PCI), which was organized by members of the Thanh Nien and activists in Hanoi, Hue, and Saigon.

WORLD WAR II AND THE FORMATION OF VIETNAM

In 1940 France signed an armistice with Germany, establishing the rule of the Vichy government, and Japan invaded Indochina for the first time. Seeing an opportunity, Ho Chi Minh returned secretly to

Indochina in January 1941, then returned to South China, where he organized the Viet Nam Doc Lap Dong Minh Hoi (League for the Independence of Vietnam), popularly known as the Viet Minh.

Notebook from Prison

Imprisoned by Chiang Kai-shek for eighteen months in 1941–1942, Ho wrote *Notebook from Prison*, a collection of short poems written in classical Chinese using a traditional Vietnamese verse form. Beginning with the line "It is your body which is in prison/Not your mind," the collection describes prison life and calls out for revolution.

In 1945 the Japanese overran Indochina and imprisoned or executed all the French officials. Ho contacted the United States forces and began to collaborate with the Office of Strategic Services against the Japanese. At the same time Viet Minh guerrillas fought the Japanese in the mountains of South China while groups of commandos began to move toward the Vietnamese capital of Hanoi.

Japan surrendered to the Allies on August 14, 1945. The Viet Minh entered Hanoi on August 19. Two weeks later Ho Chi Minh declared Vietnamese independence to an enormous crowd in Ba Dinh Square.

Independence wasn't that simple. An Allied treaty with Chiang Kai-shek gave the Chinese Nationalists the right to replace the Japanese north of the Sixteenth Parallel. Not surprisingly, liberated France, under the leadership of General Charles de Gaulle, had no intention of giving up Indochina without a fight.

The French quickly recaptured South Vietnam and began negotiations with Ho Chi Minh. Neither side was satisfied with the final agreement, which recognized Vietnam as an independent state with its own government, army, and finances, integrated into a French union controlled by Paris.

The uneasy peace flared into war in November 1946, when a French cruiser opened fire on the town of Haiphong after a clash between French and Vietnamese soldiers. By the end of 1953 most of the countryside was under Viet Minh control and the country's larger cities were under siege. The French defeat at Dien Bien Phu in 1954 ended France's Southeast Asian empire.

Ho and American Independence

Was Ho Chi Minh familiar with the Declaration of Independence? Very likely. The words Ho used to announce Vietnam's independence sound very similar to Thomas Jefferson's: "All men are born equal: the Creator has given us inviolable rights: life, liberty and happiness."

VIETNAM DIVIDED

The Geneva Accords, signed on July 21, 1954, divided Vietnam at the Seventeenth Parallel, creating a communist state in the north, led by Ho Chi Minh, and an anti-communist state in the south, led by Ngo Dinh Diem. The division of Vietnam created a Cold War battlefront, with the United States supporting Ngo Dinh Diem and the Soviet Union, and the People's Republic of China providing aid to Ho Chi Minh.

The Accords called for a 1956 election that would reestablish a unified Vietnam. When the time came for the elections, South Vietnam refused to play, setting the stage for the United States' entry into the Vietnam War.

THE ANTIWAR MOVEMENT IN THE US

Although most Americans remained relatively unaware of their country's growing involvement in Vietnam, by the middle of the 1960s one factor had changed this significantly: television. Night after night, images of young men at war were broadcast. As President Lyndon Johnson relied more and more on the draft to create a steady supply of soldiers whom he could send to Vietnam, resistance steadily grew. By 1967 the movement against the war had taken shape and begun to vigorously express itself.

The 1967 Marches

In 1967 two massive protests of the war occurred. The first, in April, was held in New York, where some 400,000 people marched from Central Park to the United Nations. At the second, held in Washington, DC, in October, marchers attempted to encircle the Pentagon.

In 1968 protests against the war turned violent at the Democratic National Convention. In what was later described in an official report as a "police riot," Chicago police beat demonstrators and reporters. In the words of some, the war had come home.

Although Johnson and his successor, Richard Nixon, publicly claimed not to be influenced by the protests, internal documents of both administrations show they were deeply concerned by them. Equally distressing to them was the fact that the protest activity was exposing many young people to more radical notions about what was wrong with society. Socialist organizations in the 1960s and early 1970s showed a steady growth, primarily from people disillusioned by the war.

SOCIALISM AND THE "NEW LEFT"

Rediscovery of Socialism

Socialism enjoyed a brief resurgence in America in the 1960s and early 1970s. A New Left emerged from the interaction between the civil rights movement and the socialist movement of the 1930s (which became known as the Old Left), as well as protests against the Vietnam War. Composed largely of college students, the New Left refused to be drawn into the communist–anti-communist dichotomy that characterized the Old Left. Their initial concerns were racism and poverty, but these quickly took a back seat to protests against the Vietnam War. The movement peaked in the mid-1960s and had virtually disappeared by the mid-1970s.

SDS

The most well-known New Left organization was Students for a Democratic Society (SDS). Founded in 1960 as a student affiliate of the League for Industrial Democracy, SDS quickly broke away from the Marxist dogmatism of its founding organization.

In 1962 the SDS held a national convention in Port Huron, Michigan, to create its own operating manifesto. After several days of discussion the society adopted the Port Huron Statement, written for the most part by University of Michigan student newspaper editor Tom Hayden, who later rose to national prominence as one of the eight young men charged with inciting riots around the 1968

Democratic National Convention. The manifesto drew on a range of socialist and political traditions, from the town hall meeting to Marx. The statement began with a critique of American society that dealt with race relations, the persistence of poverty, and America's role in the Cold War. It then outlined the organization's vision of reform based on a loosely defined concept of "participatory democracy."

Participatory Democracy

The SDS idea of "participatory democracy" grew out of the writings of John Dewey, as elaborated by University of Michigan professor Arnold Kaufman. The basic idea, as expressed by Dewey, is that "all those who are affected by social institutions must have a share in producing and managing them."

SDS grew slowly until 1965, when the United States' involvement in the Vietnam War escalated. In 1962 the group had roughly three hundred members; estimates of the organization's membership at its highest point range from 30,000 to 100,000. After the party organized a mass antiwar march on Washington in April 1965, the organization grew more militant: staging student strikes and occupying university administration buildings.

At its 1969 convention the organization disintegrated as the result of a power struggle between the Revolutionary Youth Movement and the Progressive Labor Party. Members of the Revolutionary Youth Movement expelled the more moderate faction from the party. A number of members unaffiliated with either faction resigned in disgust, leaving the party in the hands of its most radical element. Soon thereafter, the remaining members transformed themselves into the violent revolutionary group, the Weathermen.

REACTION

Reaganism and Neoliberalism

The election of Ronald Reagan as president of the United States signaled a sharp turn to the right in American politics. Reagan found a kindred spirit in the UK's Margaret Thatcher, and both of them set out to privatize those segments of their economies that had been nationalized.

NEOLIBERALISM

To a large extent both Reagan and Thatcher found inspiration in the ideas of Adam Smith, the eighteenth-century economist whose central tenet was the "invisible hand" of the marketplace. Smith's twentieth-century followers argued that less government was better and the smaller the role government played in the economy, the healthier the nation's economic situation would become. Reagan summed up his views in the statement "Government is not the solution to our problem; government *is* the problem."

Socialists had argued that the role of government was to administer a fair distribution of economic resources. Neoliberals argued that the process occurred naturally, without the intervention of government. While socialists suggested that higher taxes, particularly on the wealthy, could help pay the cost of social programs such as healthcare and education, neoliberals retorted that lowering taxes accomplished two ends:

- It put more money in the hands of working people, allowing them to increase spending and thus create more jobs.

- It put more money in the hands of wealthy people, the real job creators. If the tax burden on the rich and corporations was reduced, neoliberals argued, the result would be a "trickle-down effect." Money given to the top echelons of society would trickle down to the bottom through increased job creation.

The Chicago School

Among the most enthusiastic supporters of neoliberalism was Milton Friedman (1912–2006), a professor of economics at the University of Chicago. Friedman argued that the most important measure of a country's economic health was the rate at which the money supply was increasing. When the government of Chile fell to a military coup, led by General Augusto Pinochet, in late 1973, Friedman (among others) became an advisor to the Chilean dictatorship. The result was a series of moves that enriched Chile's elites while impoverishing the working class. It was the Pinochet government's policies that enshrined the word *neoliberalism* in economists' vocabularies.

Reaganism in Practice

Reagan put this doctrine into practice in the 1990s in the United States. While the economy experienced growth, there were two significant consequences:

1. Military spending increased vastly due to the administration's emphasis on defense.
2. The national deficit ballooned. Neoliberals argued that the deficit (the difference between what the government spends and what it takes in) didn't matter, since it would shortly start to go down because of economic growth. This didn't happen, and Reagan added $1.4 trillion in deficits.

REAGAN CONSERVATISM

During the 1990s in the United States and elsewhere conservatism was on the rise. Although there was no McCarthyite witch hunt, as in the 1950s, voters generally preferred conservative candidates and rejected any suggestion of liberalism. This was helped by the fact that Reagan used his acting skills to present conservative thought with a cheerful facade. Even events such as the invasion and overthrow of the leftist government of Grenada in 1983 and the secret US support for anti-leftist guerrillas in Nicaragua in the mid to late 1980s did little to blunt the positive spin Reagan was able to put on the battle against socialist ideas. This was helped by the collapse of the Soviet Union in 1989, an event that occurred in the administration of Reagan's successor, George H.W. Bush, but one for which he was largely given credit.

Socialist Movements in Europe

Despite the lack of interest in socialism in the United States in the 1980s and 1990s, it remained a popular political strain in European politics. Socialist parties were still significant forces in the parliaments of France and elsewhere. At the same time ultra-conservative movements also arose, often in response to non-European immigration. These included the skinheads in the UK and the National Front in France led by Jean-Marie Le Pen.

The result of all this was that socialist ideas in the United States in the last decade of the twentieth century seemed to have died away. The New Left collapsed in the 1970s, and very little organized socialist activity remained.

SOCIALISTS AND THE GREEN MOVEMENT

A New Deal

The fundamental idea behind Green socialism is that our industrial system, and the ideas about our place in the natural world that accompany it, are rapidly destroying the planet. The endless spiral of new needs and wants has led to demands for greater quantities of material goods and comforts. The political systems of the West, socialist and nonsocialist alike, have worked to expand production capacity. Traditionally, the socialist debate focused on how to distribute the products of industrial society more equitably. Green socialists have moved the debate to the amount and quality of what is being consumed and the kind of workday needed to produce it.

Green socialist thought rests on the work of political philosopher Herbert Marcuse and other social theorists of the Frankfurt School. Marcuse questioned the Marxist idea of *homo faber*: the concept that humans are primarily working beings who create themselves through their labor. He argued that true freedom is realized through the instinctual forces of *eros*, or passion, and playful activity. Work requires the renunciation of instinctual pleasure. Alienated from *eros* by the discipline of work, the majority of the working classes have come to believe that freedom means having more and better consumer goods. While the elevation of work over *eros* was necessary in times of economic scarcity, Marcuse claimed this should no longer be a problem in highly developed societies. Society's challenge is to use technology to provide basic goods and services in a way that would allow everyone to bridge the gap between work and meaningful play.

Green socialists analyze the economic and political roots of the environmental crisis in terms of Marcuse's critique of *homo faber*, mass culture, and consumerism. Their proposed solutions take two basic forms: an "eco-state" that would play a major role in protecting the environment, and a loose federation of self-governing and largely self-sufficient communes.

Marx and Freud

German-born political philosopher Herbert Marcuse (1898–1979) used Freud's theories of psychoanalysis to critique Marxism. His most important works, *Eros and Civilization: A Philosophical Inquiry into Freud* (1955) and *One-Dimensional Man* (1964), were influential in the leftist student movements of the 1960s in both Europe and the United States.

RUDOLF BAHRO

Green philosopher and activist Rudolf Bahro (1935–1997) wrote one of the most powerful ecological critiques of Marxism in *The Alternative in Eastern Europe* (1977). He pointed out that Marx assumed that socialism would be a *classless* industrial society but an industrial society nonetheless. Instead, Bahro argued that humanity needed "not only to transform its relations of production, but must also fundamentally transform the entire character of its mode of production." Consumption is an inherent part of capitalism, which creates unnecessary and wasteful commodities at the expense of needs in its pursuit of profit. In order to reduce consumption, and industry's damage to the environment, it is necessary to transform society.

Bahro suggested a "communist alternative" to state socialism that he described as Green anarcho-communism. In addition to changing the "relations of production," socialists needed to change humanity's relationship with the environment, creating a new economy geared toward producing no more than is needed for subsistence. In addition to reducing damage to the environment, scaling down needs would allow a massive reduction in the number of hours spent working.

Bahro and the Communist Party

Rudolf Bahro joined the East Germany Communist Party at seventeen. He withdrew his membership following the Soviet invasion of Czechoslovakia in 1968. As a result of *The Alternative in Eastern Europe*, he was imprisoned for two years and then deported to West Germany. He was a founding member of the West German Green Party, from which he subsequently resigned.

Because small-scale technology could not satisfy the needs of large urban populations, people should create federations of communes that could produce 90 percent of what they need, deal on a national level for another 9 percent, and for the last 1 percent deal with a world market.

ANDRÉ GORZ

André Gorz (1923–2007) argued that most people are stifled within the world of work. Most jobs are both boring and enslaving. Technological innovation and automation created a situation in which there is increasingly less work for people, but capitalism did not provide a framework for allowing people to work less. Consequently, the unemployed do not have the resources to enjoy a decent life, and the employed do not have the time. Gorz proposed a combination of lower consumption, a reduced workweek, and a guaranteed minimum income that would allow people to pursue independent activities, including socially useful pursuits that would benefit others.

Gorz drew a distinction between *environmentalism* and what he called *ecologism*. Environmentalism limits itself to a call for renewable sources of energy, recycling, and preservation. Ecologism demands an end to the fetishism of commodities and consumption.

SOCIALISM AND THE FUTURE

What Will It Bring?

For many Americans, their most dramatic exposure to socialism came during the 2016 presidential election. Senator Bernie Sanders, an avowed democratic socialist, ran a widely popular campaign for the Democratic Party nomination. Although unsuccessful, he made millions of people aware of, and in many cases accepting of, the concepts of democratic socialism.

FEEL THE BERN!

Bernie Sanders (1941–), although representing Vermont, was born in Brooklyn. As a young man he was involved in the civil rights movement, which had a significant political impact on him. He later moved to Vermont, where he ran several unsuccessful campaigns for political office before being elected mayor of the city of Burlington in 1981. He was later elected to the House of Representatives and then, in 2005, to the US Senate.

Sanders is an independent, although he caucuses with the Democratic Party. He argues for largely following the Scandinavian model of socialism, including universal healthcare and education, and for substantially increasing taxes on large corporations and wealthy individuals. He is also a strong advocate for campaign finance reform.

During the Great Recession of 2008–2010 Sanders was one of the voices calling for the breakup of the large banks and investment firms that traded in unstable securities. He supports raising the minimum wage to $15 an hour and has also spoken on behalf of bills that would make joining unions easier.

In 2019 Sanders announced that he would again campaign for the Democratic nomination for president. Although his campaign in 2016 was unsuccessful, he made clear that an openly democratic socialist can garner a great deal of support.

SOCIALISTS ELECTED

Bernie Sanders is not the only American socialist to hold political office in the early twenty-first century. In 2013 Kshama Sawant won a seat on the Seattle City Council. Sawant is a member of Socialist Alternative, a socialist organization with Trotskyist origins.

Sawant ran on a program advocating a minimum wage of $15 an hour (something that was passed into law by the City Council and took effect in 2015), rent control, and higher taxes on local corporations, such as Boeing, Microsoft, and Amazon. Unlike Bernie Sanders, she rejected working through the Democratic Party and has maintained her independence from it.

Anna Louise Strong

Another Seattle socialist, albeit from an earlier time, was Anna Louise Strong, a reporter and social activist who served on the Seattle School Board in 1916. Strong later reported on the newly formed Soviet Union and other events from around the globe.

DEMOCRATIC SOCIALISTS
OF AMERICA

By far the largest socialist organization in America today is the Democratic Socialists of America. It was formed through a series of splits and mergers. In the 1970s a group split off from the Socialist Party of America, which it felt had moved too far to the right, and formed the Democratic Socialist Organizing Committee. In 1982 it merged with the New American Movement, a group with roots in the Old Left, to form the Democratic Socialists of America.

As of the end of 2018 the DSA has more than fifty thousand members (the last socialist organization in the United States to claim such numbers was the Communist Party in the 1930s, which had more than 100,000 members). A number of its members have been elected to office, including a member of the Virginia House of Delegates and two women to the US House of Representatives: Alexandria Ocasio-Cortez and Rashida Tlaib.

Michael Harrington

Among the DSA's earliest leaders was Michael Harrington (1928–1989). Harrington, a longtime member of the Socialist Party, was the author of *The Other America*, a study of poverty in the United States published in 1962. The book shocked many since the issue of poverty, not only in areas of the rural south but in the larger cities of the north, had been largely ignored up to that time.

ALEXANDRIA OCASIO-CORTEZ
(1989–)

Ocasio-Cortez has become one of the most prominent voices of socialism in the United States today—partly by virtue of the number of attacks launched against her by conservative commentators. Born in the Bronx in New York, she graduated from Boston University and worked a number of jobs to support herself and her mother. She was a volunteer for Bernie Sanders's 2016 presidential campaign and traveled around the United States talking to people about the problems they face. When elected to Congress, she was the youngest person ever to hold the position of Representative.

Positions

Ocasio-Cortez is best known for her advocacy of Medicare for All, an attempt to massively expand healthcare in the United States, and the Green New Deal. This is a series of measures, spread out over ten years, that aims to make the US more energy efficient and to cut carbon emissions in an effort to fight global warming.

The face of socialism has changed many times over the years. In people such as Ocasio-Cortez, it seems to have found a new face for the twenty-first century.

Socialist Surge in Chicago

In the 2019 elections for city council in Chicago, six democratic socialists were elected as aldermen. All were supported by the DSA.

INDEX

ABOUT THE AUTHOR

Kathleen Sears has a wide array of interests and enjoys taking a deep dive into new subject matter. She is the author of *American Government 101*, *Mythology 101*, *US History 101*, *Grammar 101*, and *Weather 101*.

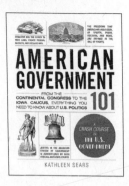